D1379104

La Maison du Chocolat

La Maison du Chocolat

TIMELESS CLASSICS WITH A TWIST

Gilles Marchal

PHOTOGRAPHS BY
Véronique Durruty

Stewart, Tabori & Chang

NEW YORK

CONTENTS

Pure chocolate etc.

Timeless Classics

Playful Uses for Chocolate

Sprinkled with Salt

Stunning Creations

Practical Information

The Magic of Chocolate

"Eat chocolate and even the worst company seems good," wrote Madame de Sévigné to her daughter. More recently, pianist and master of improvisation Martial Solal admitted that, like many jazz musicians, he could not pick up his instrument until he had partaken of a magical substance: in his case, a piece of chocolate, "the food of the gods" (*Theobroma*). Hovering between playful and magical, ethereal charm and material decadence, memory (of childhood) and imagination, the secrets of a science and the mysteries of an art (refined over seven years in the *pâtisserie* "laboratories" at the Crillon, Prunier, the Plaza Athénée, and finally Le Bristol), this book presents an irresistible collection—or rather a polyptych—of thirty-six original masterpieces by Gilles Marchal, who is now head of the temple of chocolate, La Maison du Chocolat, founded by Robert Linxe in 1977. Nine years after the release of the first anthology of expertise (Robert Linxe, *La Maison du Chocolat,* Paris, Le Chêne, 2000), this second publication could be described as a luxurious catalogue of this gallery or exhibition, offering an exquisite sampler that lacks only the flavors themselves. Gilles Marchal has adopted and masterfully updated the now-legendary legacy of La Maison du Chocolat, producing a culinary tour de force that is appetizing to both the eyes and the palate. Elegance and visual appeal are always at the forefront in his delectable creations. He has honed his passion into an exquisite paradox, like the proverbial silence following a Mozart concerto that sounds as if it were also composed by Mozart; in this case, the world of chocolate is still ever present even after the flavor of the chocolate has faded away. To bring this compelling illusion to life, Gilles invited six talented young artists—Camille Lescure, Claire Colin, Mona Oren, Élodie Rousselot, Camille Hammerer, and Vanessa Batut—to invent and improvise shapes, images, and objects associated with or made from items that are inseparable from chocolate and its illustrious Maison, from the source of the cocoa to the most fleeting yet unforgettable culinary creations. The end result is a fascinating compilation that takes the fairy-tale world of chocolate above and beyond La Maison du Chocolat. Yet one of the book's greatest charms is that the wonderful world of chocolate, as transfigured by Gilles Marchal, is finally accessible to ardent foodies and amateurs alike. The chef methodically reveals, in great detail, the magic formulas, tips, and procedures home chefs require to replicate the miracles and conjuring tricks that he modestly calls "recipes." Sorcerer's apprentices, to your ganache bowls!

—Michèle Carles

On the **cocoa** trail

Pleasure, happiness, discovery, sensitivity, and joy are the words that have motivated me every day for the past twenty years as I create new sensations through the subtle balance of flavors, the essence of all my sweet and savory inventions.

"Finding pleasure in giving pleasure" is how I would define my magnificent profession (and art): master pastry chef, chocolatier, confectioner, and ice cream maker. It was the first qualification I earned in my native Lorraine at the age of seventeen. This passion for flavor was a gift from a true master, Claude Bourguignon, when I was his apprentice in Metz. He was the one who, when I left for Paris, whispered in my ear, "There is one place you absolutely must visit: La Maison du Chocolat."

But it was my parents and our countless family meals, when it was completely natural to spend hours over a hot stove, that taught me about taste and instilled in me a desire to seek out new flavors every day.

To me, flavor is a complex culture that has to be revisited each day. After a few wonderful years with Pit Oberweis, the greatest pastry chef in Luxembourg, who gave me the confidence I needed for my very first creations, I began to jump from one prestigious Parisian establishment to the next: Le Crillon hotel with Christophe Felder and Christian Constant; the restaurant Prunier Traktir with Gabriel Biscay; the Plaza Athénée hotel as pastry chef with Éric Briffard, and finally Le Bristol hotel alongside Éric Fréchon, one of the greatest chefs I know, with whom I spent eight years sharing our mutual passion: a true life of luxury.

And then we come to 1985, when I finally discovered these chocolate gems and their exotic flavors: the year I first set foot in La Maison du Chocolat on Rue du Faubourg-Saint-Honoré. The boutique and its location were magical. After several encounters here and there with Robert Linxe over the years, he eventually bestowed on me the honor of creating for the remarkable Maison du Chocolat, a member of the Comité Colbert. This place will always be an international standard in gourmet luxury.

Since I arrived at La Maison du Chocolat, I have not stopped discovering new spices, teas, herbs or plants, and cocoas on every trip, which are tested and then often added to a ganache or dessert to give it subtle flavor. Today and tomorrow, La Maison du Chocolat gives me the opportunity to express my creative passion to the fullest through the never-ending exploration of new horizons of flavor and freshness.

Art is born of creation

With each passing day, I grow more and more motivated to share my experiences. At La Maison du Chocolat, learning a skill and passing it on are one and the same. After studying and mastering the great classics of French pastry and chocolate making, I decided to modernize them for La Maison du Chocolat by retaining and enhancing their original flavors.

Through this book, I hope to share my expertise with you as you make both traditional recipes and unusual creations, always presented with artistry and innovation, but, more importantly, in a way that respects textures, fragrances, and flavors so that you remember a dish for its delicious taste before its luscious look.

Sharing my creations with artists has become a natural extension of my work. I fell in love with this kind of interaction instantly, the way the artists' passion fueled my creativity. They used their favorite materials to produce the art of handicraft so dear to La Maison du Chocolat. Yet I am merely the instigator of these recipes. I had the enormous privilege of working closely with the artists for several months as they added new depths of meaning and a common thread to the book. Art was produced in all its forms: table decoration, jewelry, from sculpture to braiding and, to crown it all, photography.

Through the expert lens of Véronique Durruty, my chocolate creations are magically transformed into true masterpieces of sculpture. Véronique captures not just the sensations and the colors, but also the flavors of my creations—we are the perfect team, seamlessly making the eye, hand, and palate as one.

My recipes, shot in natural daylight, were made using the finest chocolate.

They are revealed to you here, in this book, exactly as we imagined them. Congratulations and thanks to the artists!

—Gilles Marchal

We have known for a long time that food is enjoyed just as much with the eyes and nose as with the mouth. Yet people still tend to see photographs as purely visual illustrations, as though they were shut off from the other senses. My artistic work is a journey through the senses and sensations: I produce tactile photos, fragrant photos, photos that whisper. If it were possible, I would want people to look at my photos with their eyes closed in order to feel them more intensely.

I have worked with many artists whose creations affect other senses: I have explored touch, asked musicians to compose music inspired by my photos, and encouraged leading noses to create perfumes based on my images. A chance to explore the taste buds was truly tempting! But I am not a food photographer. When the publisher offered me this assignment, I was of two minds. After all, there are already so many books on the subject—and all so similar.

But then I met Gilles Marchal. He talked to me about his creative process. His eyes sparkled when he spoke about flavor; just the way he described choosing the right ingredients made my mouth water. He explained certain vintages of chocolate as though they were fine wines, and in a way that spoke to all the senses; he wanted to make his readers want to lick the pages of his book. I was already won over. Then he told me that he would share all of his secrets, divulging the genuine recipes and any tips readers would need to make them at home, just as good as the originals.

We got to work right away: no stylists, no studio, no filters, no flash. A feast for the eyes and the palate. After each photo shoot, I was lucky enough to get to eat the subject! Gilles' inventiveness, generosity, and *joie de vivre* shine through in every one of his creations. He made the recipes at my house, on the day of each shoot, in my kitchen, so I know that all the recipes in this book can be made in a typical residential kitchen. And all of the photos show the actual results: no false textures have been added to make the food look better for the picture. So if at first you don't succeed in making a dish that is as appealing or as impressive as those pictured here, rest assured that we haven't cheated. Just try, try again! Isn't that all part of the fun?

—Véronique Durruty

Pure
chocolate
etc.

Camille Lescure

Textile designer and creator Camille Lescure uses an artistic approach that draws on a wide range of materials, both traditional and modern. In her decidedly couture style, she assembles, embroiders, weaves, and crochets metal, silk, leather, and other materials. "Anything can be used in design as long as it provokes and awakens the imagination, our inner poetry, dreams, and desires, highlighting the body's sensuality," she says. Halfway between a breastplate and a piece of jewelry, *Déjà au ciel, divine marquise* decorates the body with inspiration drawn from unique, timeless worlds. You can imagine this piece adorning a courtesan for the great pleasure of her master.

The slender neckpiece combines ribbons from chocolate boxes, diverted from their original purpose and crocheted with silk thread. The neck opening is crowned with circles of black, chocolate-box paper joined together to resemble lace flounces. Smaller pieces of the paper are crocheted together to cascade down the front of the piece in a frothy black jabot. The center of the neck is adorned with coppery leather buds nestled between metal shells. Crystals cast light on the natural cocoa beans, daring viewers to take a bite.

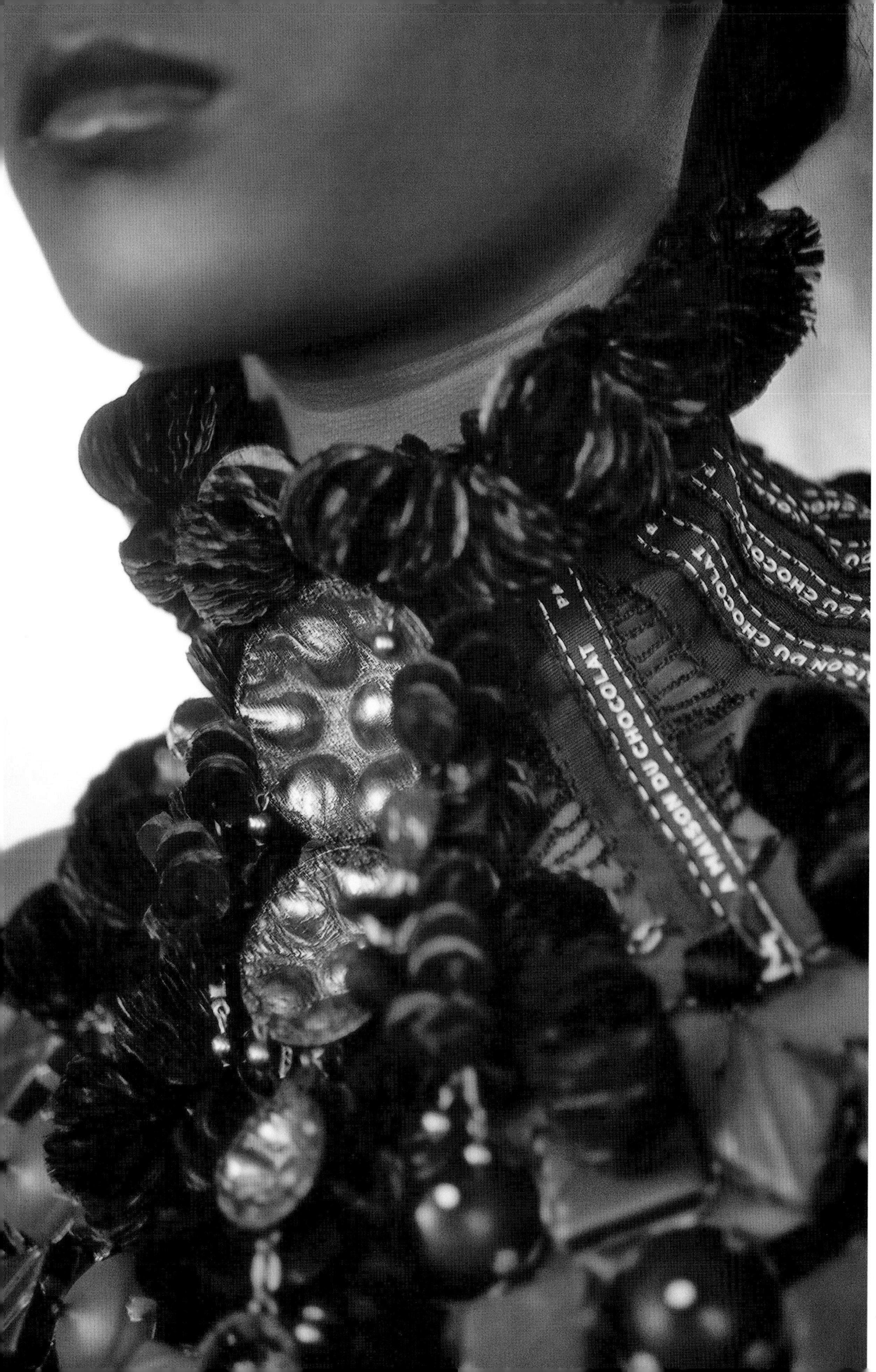
MAISON DU CHOCOLAT

A **Light Truffle** along the **Cocoa Route**

Makes 50 truffles

Preparation time: **1 hour 30 minutes**

Resting time: **1 hour**

Cooking time: **10 minutes**

FROM THE **STORES**

For the truffle filling (ganache mousse)

9 oz (250 g) dark chocolate 60% cocoa

½ cup + 2 tablespoons (150 ml) heavy cream

4 tablespoons (30 g) unsalted butter

Finishing touches

1½ cups (125 g) unsweetened cocoa powder

3½ oz (100 g) dark chocolate 70% cocoa

KITCHEN UTENSILS

Whisk

Piping bag with No. 8 or No. 10 (⁵⁄₁₆ or ⅜ in)
    round tip

Fine-mesh strainer

Plastic box, about 8 × 4 in (20 × 10 cm)

Wax paper and plastic wrap

DIRECTIONS

**For the truffle filling
(ganache mousse)**

▣ Finely chop the chocolate and set aside in a mixing bowl. In a saucepan, bring the heavy cream to a boil. Pour it over the chocolate. Leave the chocolate to melt for 2 minutes, then whisk lightly in small circles, starting from the center. When the ganache thickens, move the whisk toward the sides of the bowl until you obtain a smooth texture. Add the butter in small pieces and stir gently until it has melted completely; you should be left with a silky, glossy ganache. Cover with plastic wrap and chill for approximately 45 minutes. Stir occasionally; the texture should be lighter than a traditional ganache.

Using the fine-mesh strainer, sift the cocoa into the plastic box.

▣ Place a sheet of wax paper (approximately 12 × 8 in or 30 × 20 cm) in a dish that can be refrigerated. Remove the ganache from the refrigerator and beat vigorously; it should become lighter in color and texture.

Use the piping bag to form walnut-size ganache balls on the wax paper. Refrigerate the truffles for approximately 1 hour.

Finishing touches

▣ Melt the dark chocolate in a bain-marie to approximately 95°F/35°C. Spread a small amount of the melted chocolate into the palm of your hand and roll the truffles one by one to coat them with a thin layer of chocolate—kids will love getting their hands dirty! Place the truffles immediately into the cocoa, and shake the box back and forth to coat them thoroughly with the powder.

▣ Using a fork, if it will help, remove the truffles carefully and arrange on a plate.

▣ Store your truffles in an airtight container in the bottom of the refrigerator. Enjoy them over the next few days.

A **word** from **Gilles** Marchal

A dance step? A mushroom? No, this truffle is one that sweet tooths young and old can enjoy. The truffle was invented in the nineteenth century by Maître Dufour, a confectioner from Chambery, France. There's a truffle for every palate: flavored with aged brandy, vanilla, praline, fruit pulp, or spices. Some truffles are coated in chocolate, some are not—but a cocoa-powder coating is essential. Do you prefer white truffles or dark truffles? At La Maison du Chocolat, all of our truffles are dark—but we come up with new recipes all the time.

Hot Chocolate with Tricolor Spiced Cigarettes

Serves 6

Preparation time: **1 hour 30 minutes**

Cooking time: **30 minutes**

For the hot chocolate

¼ orange

7½ oz (200 g) dark chocolate 70% cocoa

3 slices gingerbread, preferably pain
   de mie

1 tablespoon pine honey

3 cups (750 ml) whole milk

1 cup (250 ml) heavy cream

¼ cup (20 g) unsweetened cocoa
   powder

**For the vanilla, cocoa, and
spiced cigarettes**

6 tablespoons (90 g) unsalted butter

⅔ cup (80 g) confectioners' sugar

¾ cup (90 g) cake flour

3 egg whites (about 3 oz/90 g)

½ Bourbon vanilla bean

3 pinches ground cinnamon

6 teaspoons (10 g) unsweetened cocoa
   powder

Presentation

1¾ oz (50 g) dark chocolate 60% cocoa

¾ cup + 1 tablespoon (200 ml)
   whole milk, cold

KITCHEN UTENSILS

6 clear glasses or teacups

Nonstick silicone mat or parchment
   paper

Plastic stencil, 5 × 4 × ¹⁄₃₂ in (12 cm ×
   10 cm × 1 mm), cut out of a plastic lid

Hand-held immersion blender

Microplane grater

Fine-mesh strainer or cheesecloth

Wooden spoon with round handle

Stainless steel decorating spatula or
   knife with long blade

DIRECTIONS

For the hot chocolate

◉ Zest the orange. Finely chop the chocolate and set aside in a mixing bowl. Place the gingerbread, cut into small pieces, in a saucepan; add the honey, milk, and heavy cream and bring to a boil. Remove from the heat and add the orange zest. Pour the warm mixture over the chocolate. Leave to melt for 2 minutes, then beat vigorously. Strain the mixture and pour it back into the saucepan, then warm over medium heat until it thickens slightly. Set aside.

**For the three types of
cigarette batter**

◉ In a mixing bowl, cream the butter until it is very soft, almost liquid. Add the sifted flour and sifted confectioners' sugar, then the egg whites. Whisk gently to obtain a smooth, glossy batter. Divide into three equal portions. Flavor one portion with the vanilla seeds scraped from the pod, one with the cinnamon, and the third with the sifted cocoa. Set aside at room temperature.

◉ Preheat the oven to 355°F/180°C. I recommend making three-color cigarettes. Place the plastic stencil on the nonstick sheet. Inside the stencil, place 3 small spoonfuls of each type of batter (vanilla, spiced, and cocoa) in a line. Spread thinly to ¹⁄₃₂ in (1 mm) using the spatula, relying on the stencil to make it uniform; the three types of batter should overlap and resemble a flag. Bake for 6 to 8 minutes. It is best not to bake too many at once so that you have time to roll them while still hot, which prevents them from breaking. ◉ Remove cookies from the oven and roll around the wooden spoon handle, leaving a portion unrolled. Set aside in an airtight container in a dry place.

Presentation

◉ Warm the chocolate, then pour into glasses or teacups. Using a hand whisk, froth the cold milk. Spoon a little of the foam onto the hot chocolate. Serve this ambrosia with the three-color cigarettes. You can serve this hot chocolate velouté with a small pitcher of hot milk to make it runnier, depending on your own taste.

A **word** from **Gilles** Marchal

Paulo Coelho loved coming to Le Bristol hotel for this hot chocolate. I even created a special recipe for him: hot chocolate flavored with orange peel, which he refers to in his book *Zahir*. For La Maison du Chocolat, I invented new recipes, including my favorite, a mixture of peppers from various origins.

For special occasions, or as a treat, run melted dark chocolate down the inside of a glass, as shown in the photo. Let the runnels harden before pouring in your hot chocolate.

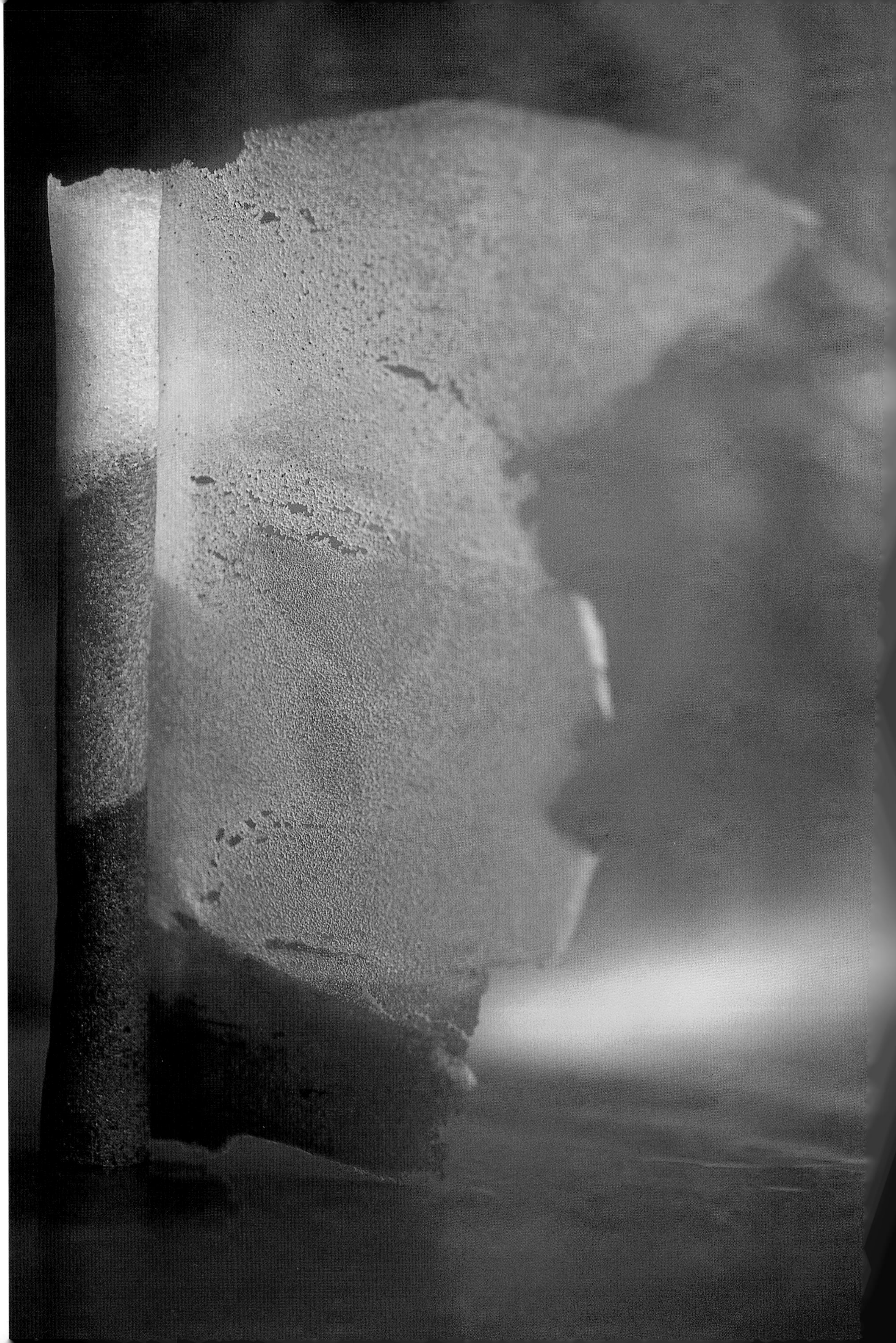

Constellation of **Caramels** and **Creamy Passion Fruit** with **Chocolate**

Makes 8 servings of cream and approximately
100 caramels

Preparation time: **40 minutes for the**
           caramels
           40 minutes for the cream

Resting time: **2 hours for the cream**

Cooking time: **35 minutes**

FROM THE **STORES**

For the chocolate–passion fruit cream

7 oz (200 g) dark chocolate 60% cocoa

½ cup + 2 tablespoons (150 ml) heavy cream

1 cup (250 ml) whole milk

7 tablespoons (100 ml) passion fruit juice

5 egg yolks (about 3½ oz/100 g)

¼ cup packed (60 g) brown sugar

For the caramels

1½ cups + 2 tablespoons (350 ml)
   heavy cream

1 Bourbon vanilla bean

2½ tablespoons (40 g) salted butter

5 pinches Guérande sea salt

1½ cups + 3 tablespoons (220 g) superfine
   granulated sugar

9 oz (250 g) glucose paste (available in
   specialty food stores or pharmacies) or
   1¼ cups (250 g) superfine granulated sugar

2 tablespoons (40 g) pine honey

¼ cup (60 ml) water

KITCHEN UTENSILS

8 small glasses

Electronic thermometer

2 stainless steel bottomless frames, about
   6 × 6 × ½ in (15 × 15 × 1.2 cm), or a square
   cake pan with straight edges lined with
   parchment paper

Cheesecloth or fine-mesh, conical strainer

100 squares (4 × 4 in or 10 × 10 cm) of bonbon
   wrapping paper (cellophane or waxed)

Parchment paper

DIRECTIONS

For the chocolate–passion fruit cream

◙ Finely chop the chocolate and set aside in a mixing bowl. In a saucepan, bring the heavy cream and milk to a boil. Add the passion fruit juice and bring back to a boil.

◙ Beat the egg yolks gently with the sugar and add to the hot liquid. Cook the mixture until it reaches a temperature of 182°F/83°C, then strain while pouring it over the chocolate. Leave to melt for 2 minutes, then whisk gently in a circular motion, working from the center outwards; this method produces a perfect emulsion, leaving the cream smooth and velvety.

◙ Divide the chocolate–passion fruit cream into small glasses, then refrigerate for 4 hours.

For the caramels

◙ Place the frame on a sheet of parchment paper, or line the bottom of your cake pan. In a saucepan, bring the cream to a boil with the vanilla (split lengthwise, and seeds scraped), butter, and salt. Remove from the heat.

◙ In another saucepan, cook the sugar, glucose paste, and honey with the water, without mixing, to the precise temperature of 302°F/150°C—reaching the last few degrees may take some time.

Bring the cream back to a boil, then remove from the heat and pour over the caramel in several additions, straining it as you go (watch out for spattering). Heat the entire mixture again until it reaches 252°F/122°C.

Pour the still-boiling caramel into the baking frame or cake pan, filling it to the top. Leave to cool completely at room temperature.

◙ Remove the frame or pan by running the blade of a large knife between the caramel and the inside of the frame or pan. Slice into strips, about ½ in (10 to 15 mm) wide, then cut the strips into small cubes about ½ in (10 and 15 mm). After they have cooled completely, wrap the caramels in individual wrappers. Enjoy them with the chocolate–passion fruit cream.

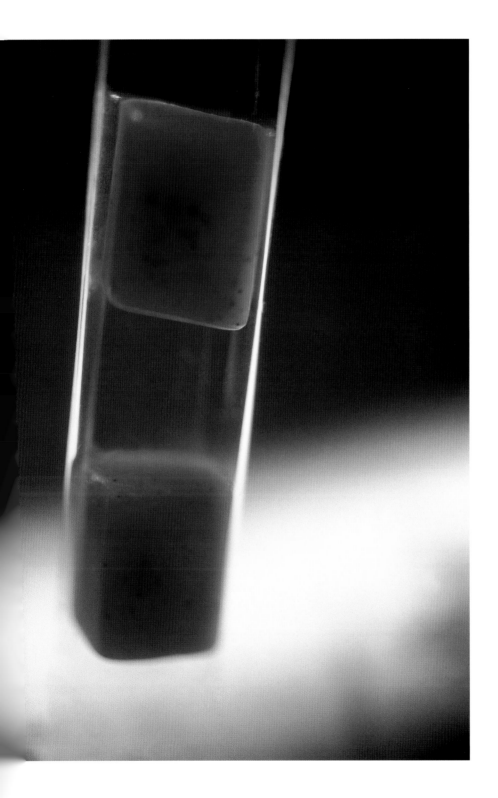

A **word** from
Gilles Marchal

This simple yet dainty recipe will whisk you back to your childhood. The sugar melts, thickens, and darkens, finally achieving the color and fragrant aromas of vanilla and warm caramel that will drive your sense of smell wild. You can replace the passion fruit juice in the chocolate cream with orange juice and serve it warm. Use a wooden skewer to dip the candies in this luscious cream.

Citrus and Curry Fruit Jelly Crystals

Makes 200 cubes

Preparation time: **1 hour 30 minutes**

Resting time: **2 hours**

Cooking time: **30 minutes**

FROM THE STORES

For the poached pears in syrup

½ cup + 2 tablespoons (150 ml) water

6 tablespoons (80 g) regular granulated sugar

Juice of ½ lemon

10 oz (300 g) fresh Bartlett pears

For the fruit jellies

3 tablespoons (40 ml) lemon juice

¼ cup (50 g) superfine granulated sugar

½ oz (15 g) fruit jelly or jam gelling agent
    (yellow pectin)

2¼ cups (450 g) regular granulated sugar

2½ oz (70 g) glucose paste (available from
    specialty food stores or pharmacies)

¼ oz (6 g) lime zest

0.1 oz (2 g) grapefruit zest

1 level teaspoon garam masala powder

For the crystallized cocoa

1 cup (200 g) superfine granulated sugar

6 teaspoons (10 g) unsweetened cocoa
    powder

1 teaspoon ground cinnamon

Presentation

1 basket red currants

KITCHEN UTENSILS

Blender

Very large saucepan

Electronic thermometer

Lemon juicer

Microplane grater

Plastic box with straight edges (5 × 5 in/
    12 × 12 cm)

Small bamboo skewers

Parchment paper

DIRECTIONS

For the poached pears in syrup

▣ Bring the water, sugar, lemon, and juice to a boil. Quarter the pears, scoop out the cores and peel, and put them in the liquid. Cover. Simmer for approximately 30 minutes. Leave to cool. Measure out 9 oz (1¼ cups/250 g) of pears and ¾ cup (200 ml) of the cooking juices.
Mash to a pulp.

For the fruit jellies

▣ Bring the pulp (see above) to a boil with 2 tablespoons (30 ml) of the lemon juice. In a bowl, mix the superfine granulated sugar and gelling agent dry, then pour over the warm pear purée, stirring constantly. Bring back to a boil. Add the regular granulated sugar and glucose. Heat to the precise temperature of 226°F/ 108°C, stirring occasionally (it may take a while to reach the last few degrees).
Add the zests, the remaining 1 tablespoon of lemon juice, and the curry powder. Cook for another 2 minutes to return the mixture to 226°F/108°C, then remove from the heat. Pour the boiling fruit jelly into the box lined with parchment paper to a thickness of approximately ½ in (10 to 15 mm). Leave to cool completely before cutting into ½-inch cubes (between 10 and 15 mm). Chill in the refrigerator.

For the crystallized cocoa

▣ On a plate, combine the sugar with the cocoa and cinnamon.

Presentation

▣ Dip the fruit jellies into the crystallized cocoa and roll, coating only two or three sides. Skewer the cubes and decorate with a red currant.

A **word** from **Gilles** Marchal

Try replacing the masala with another spice, such as aniseed or finely chopped fresh basil or mint. Serve with Earl Grey tea. I love to serve these sweets just before dessert. They are simply jam that has been cooked longer and "jellified." If you prefer them less sugary, you can also roll your fruit jellies in sifted cornstarch. They will look like Turkish delight, and are absolutely delicious dipped in melted chocolate.

Pure **Venezuela** for a **Dark Chocolate** Ganache

Serves 6
Preparation time: **30 minutes**
Resting time: **2 hours**
Cooking time: **10 minutes**

FROM THE **STORES**

For the dark chocolate ganache

9 oz (260 g) pure Venezuela Porcelana del
 Pedregal dark chocolate 70% cocoa
 (Valrhona), or any other Valrhona dark
 chocolate
¾ cup (200 ml) heavy cream
4 tablespoons (60 g) unsalted butter

For the milk chocolate ganache

¾ cup (200 ml) heavy cream
9 oz (250 g) milk chocolate 35% to 40%
 minimum cocoa
2 oz (50 g) dark chocolate 60% minimum
 cocoa

KITCHEN UTENSILS

Whisk

DIRECTIONS

For the dark chocolate ganache

◉ Finely chop the dark chocolate
and set aside in a mixing bowl. In a
saucepan, bring the heavy cream to
a boil. Pour it over the chocolate.
◉ Leave the chocolate to melt for
2 minutes, then whisk lightly in small
circles, starting from the center.
When the ganache thickens, move
the whisk toward the sides of the
bowl until you obtain a smooth texture. Add the butter in small pieces
and stir gently until it has melted
completely; you should be left with
a silky, glossy ganache.
◉ This mixture of two different
substances—one liquid (cream) and
the other fatty (chocolate, because it
contains cocoa butter)—is called an
emulsion. The same reaction occurs
when you make mayonnaise by mixing egg yolks and oil.

◉ You can enjoy this ganache
warm, or pour it over ice cream,
cakes, or fresh fruit. At La Maison
du Chocolat, we like to pour it into a
stainless steel frame set on a marble
slab. We leave it to solidify for 24
hours before covering it with a layer
of dark or milk couverture chocolate. The thickness of the coating
depends on the type of chocolate
we want: if thin and rounded, it
becomes a gold bar; rectangular
bars are called Caracas, Bacchus,
or Salvador; and squares go by the
names Maïko, Zagora, or Sylvia.

For the milk chocolate ganache

◉ Make the milk chocolate ganache
in the same way as the dark
chocolate ganache. Because milk
chocolate has a higher fat content
than dark chocolate (due to the
added milk), you will notice that
the recipe does not contain butter.
Instead a little dark chocolate is
added to round out the flavor of this
sweet ganache.

A **word** from **Gilles** Marchal

As a temple to ganache for more than thirty years, La Maison du Chocolat has more than a
few recipes up its sleeve! Our ganache comes flavored with Andalusian lemon zest, fresh
raspberry, Ceylon cinnamon, tea infusions, Katmandu pepper, caramelized pineapple, or
simply milk chocolate or bitter dark chocolate. The Porcelana del Pedregal plantation in
Venezuela grows a very rare bean—the *criollo,* so light in color that it was named Porcelana
(porcelain). The chocolate it produces is unique in the world, thanks to its aromas. We at La
Maison du Chocolat owe a great deal to Robert Linxe for inventing these recipes, which have
left an indelible imprint on the chocolate we produce.

Dark Chocolate **Ice Cream**

Serves 6
Preparation time: **45 minutes**
Resting time: **2 hours**
Cooking time: **10 minutes**

FROM THE **STORES**

3½ oz (100 g) dark chocolate 60% cocoa
1 cup (250 ml) whole milk
½ cup (120 ml) heavy cream
6 teaspoons (10 g) unsweetened cocoa
    powder
4 teaspoons (30 g) acacia honey
½ Bourbon vanilla bean
1 whole egg (2 oz/60 g)
2 egg yolks (1½ oz/40 g)
3 tablespoons packed (40 g) brown sugar

KITCHEN UTENSILS
Electronic thermometer
Cheesecloth or fine-mesh, conical strainer
Ice cream maker
Plastic wrap or airtight container

DIRECTIONS

◙ Finely chop the chocolate and set aside in a mixing bowl. In a saucepan, bring the whole milk and heavy cream to a boil with the cocoa, honey, and vanilla bean (split lengthwise, and seeds scraped).

◙ In a shallow bowl, mix the egg, egg yolks, and sugar until they turn a pale yellow color. Pour the mixture into a boiling liquid. Cook as you would a custard to reach a temperature of 181°F/83°C. Strain directly onto the chopped chocolate in the bowl.

◙ Leave to melt for 2 minutes, then beat together. Let the chocolate cream cool before refrigerating for 2 hours.

◙ Pour the chilled cream into an ice cream maker and freeze according to the manufacturer's instructions; it should have the recognizable smooth, creamy texture.

◙ Cover the cream with plastic wrap or place in an airtight container. Store in the freezer.

A **word** from **Gilles** Marchal

This ice cream, made using eggs, is custard based—and can actually be enjoyed as a custard, too. The custard is frozen to approximately 3°F/-16°C in an ice cream maker (there are a variety of models available to suit every type of kitchen). Store the ice cream in an airtight container in your freezer.

Try accompanying this delicious ice cream with caramelized nuts, coconut macarons, whipped cream, or bananas flambéed in aged cognac. Or simply give in to temptation and indulge in one of La Maison du Chocolat's new ice cream and sorbet flavors: Bourbon vanilla ice cream, Guérande sea salt and caramel ice cream, or poached raspberry sorbet with seeds.

Sandy Praline Clusters

Makes 60 clusters

Preparation time: **50 minutes**

Resting time: **2 hours**

Cooking time: **15 minutes**

FROM THE **STORES**

For the almond praline

7½ oz (200 g) whole blanched almonds

2 cups (200 g) finely chopped almonds

¾ cup + 2 tablespoons (170 g) superfine
   granulated sugar

3 tablespoons (50 ml) water

4 oz (120 g) milk chocolate 35% to 40% cocoa

Finishing touches

7 oz (200 g) milk chocolate 35% to 40% cocoa
   or dark chocolate 60% cocoa

KITCHEN UTENSILS

Electronic thermometer

Food processor

Dish with straight edges or plastic box, about
   5 × 5 in (12 × 12 cm)

Parchment paper and plastic wrap

DIRECTIONS

For the almond praline

◉ Preheat the oven to 320°F/160°C. Cover a baking sheet with parchment paper and arrange the whole almonds (for the almond praline) on one side and the finely chopped almonds (to coat the praline) on the other, taking care to keep them separate. Bake the almonds until they turn an even, light-brown color. The chopped almonds will be ready first: set them aside on a plate. Leave the whole almonds to cool on the parchment paper.

◉ In a saucepan, cook the sugar with the water to obtain a brown caramel. Remove from the heat, add the whole almonds, and stir to coat them completely in the caramel mixture. Spread the almonds out on the parchment paper. As they cool, they will form a sheet of nougatine. Break this up into big chunks.

Finely chop the chocolate and melt in a bain-marie, stirring from time to time and making sure the temperature never exceeds 90°F/32°C.

◉ In a food processor, pulse the caramelized almonds (chunks of nougatine) until you obtain a fine, grainy mixture. Place in a bowl, add the melted chocolate, and stir with a spatula to obtain an even consistency. Pour the mixture into the dish (or box) lined with plastic wrap to a depth of approximately ½ in (1½ cm). Leave the praline to chill for 2 hours.

Finishing touches

◉ Cover your work surface with parchment paper, then flip the dish over onto it and remove the plastic wrap. With a long, sharp knife, cut the praline into ½-inch (1½-cm) strips, then chop the other way to form cubes.

◉ Coat the praline cubes with the chopped almonds by simply rolling them gently by hand.

Chop the milk or dark chocolate and melt it in a bain-marie, making sure it never exceeds 95°F/35°C. Leave to cool to 91°F/33°C.

◉ Individually dip each cluster into the melted chocolate to coat it completely. Use a fork to remove the clusters, and let the excess chocolate drip off. Arrange the clusters carefully on parchment paper and leave them to solidify. Refrigerate in an airtight container.

A **word** from **Gilles** Marchal

There are several types of *praliné*. The filling is named after the Duke of Praslin, who had the brilliant idea of mixing nuts with cooked sugar, then blending them to produce this delicious paste. You can make a hazelnut praline by simply replacing the almonds with these nuts. Or try rolling the almond praline clusters in ground hazelnuts. The praline paste can also be flavored with citrus zest or vanilla and made using peanuts, walnuts, pistachios—or whichever nut strikes your fancy!

Timeless
Classics

ANTHURIUM MELTDOWN, CHOCOLATE VERSION

Mona Oren

Mona Oren has created a deeply sensitive piece that hints at the cycle of life/death/rebirth through the creative process itself, particularly her use of perishable materials (wax, flowers, food, etc.) in her sculptures and installations. The decay of these materials, whether natural or accelerated by the artist, is recorded in photographs and videos.

For La Maison du Chocolat, Mona has created a piece that flows, inspired by the recipe for molten cakes. These two anthurium flowers melt and transform in front of the camera, revealing the magic of chocolate as we witness its metamorphosis.

Above: Melting chocolate by Mona Oren
Opposite: Melting chocolate by Gilles Marchal

Molten Dark Chocolate Cakes with a Hint of Ginger

Makes 6 cakes

Preparation time: **40 minutes**

Resting time: **3 hours in the refrigerator**

Cooking time: **12 minutes**

FROM THE STORES

4 oz (125 g) dark chocolate 70% cocoa

8 tablespoons (114 g) unsalted butter +
    4 teaspoons (20 g) for the molds

10 g (½ oz) fresh ginger

4 eggs (about 7 oz/200 g)

½ cup + 2 tablespoons (125 g) superfine
    granulated sugar

7 tablespoons (50 g) cake flour

¼ cup packed (50 g) brown sugar

KITCHEN UTENSILS

Electronic thermometer

6 small porcelain glasses, molds, or bell-
    shaped bowls

or 6 stainless steel pastry rings (about
    2½ in (7 cm) in diameter and 1½ in (4 cm)
    high) and piping bag with No. 10 or No. 12
    (⅜ in or ½ in) round tip

Sifter or cheesecloth

Parchment paper

Plastic wrap

Microplane grater

DIRECTIONS

◉ Chop the chocolate into small pieces and melt in a bain-marie until the temperature reaches 105°F/40°C. Add the butter, cut into small pieces, and mix together. Remove the mixture from the heat and keep it at 105°F/40°C in the bain-marie.

◉ Peel the ginger and grate it very finely. In a mixing bowl, whisk the eggs with the superfine granulated sugar until they turn a pale yellow color, then add the grated ginger. Pour over the melted chocolate and butter mixture and stir well. Using a sifter or cheesecloth, sift in the flour. Cover with plastic wrap and set aside for 3 hours in the refrigerator.

◉ Preheat the oven to 400°F/200°C. To simplify the process, divide the mixture into small porcelain glasses, molds, or bell-shaped bowls (that have been greased with butter and sprinkled lightly with the brown sugar). Bake for 9 to 11 minutes, depending on the oven; a crust should form around the edge, but the cake should remain semiliquid and warm inside. Serve warm.

◉ If you would rather remove the cakes from their molds before serving, you can do the following: cut the parchment paper into six strips, each 2 in wide x 8½ in long (5 cm x 22 cm). Lightly grease the insides of the stainless steel pastry rings with butter, then line them with a strip of parchment paper. Cover the baking sheet with parchment paper as well before arranging the rings on it.

◉ Using the piping bag, fill the rings three-quarters of the way to the top (about 3 oz [80 to 90 g] per ring). Bake for 9 to 11 minutes, depending on your oven: when they are baked and removed from the rings, the cakes should form a crust around the edge, but remain semiliquid and warm inside.

A word from Gilles Marchal

Enjoy these cakes warm, served with pistachio ice cream and roasted nuts (pecans, hazelnuts, pistachios). I've been making these fabulous cakes for more than fifteen years now. You need to be very precise with the baking time. I recommend that you start by doing a test (try one or two cakes) to see how your particular oven bakes.

If you're feeling brave (or simply know what you're doing), bake the cakes just in time to serve them hot from the oven for dessert. You can also enjoy them cold the following day—if there are any left, of course! Try swapping the ginger for a rich, decadent chocolate cake. Or before baking, why not add candied orange or lemon peel, fresh raspberries . . .

Enlightening Chocolate Éclairs

Makes 15 éclairs
Preparation time: **2 hours**
Resting time: **1 hour**
Cooking time: **45 minutes**

FROM THE STORES

For the icing

4 sheets gelatine (about ½ oz/8 g)

½ cup (120 ml) water

¾ cup (150 g) superfine granulated sugar

¾ cup (60 g) unsweetened cocoa powder

7 tablespoons (100 ml) heavy cream

For the pastry cream

6¼ oz (180 g) dark chocolate 60% cocoa

1⅔ cups (400 ml) whole milk

7 tablespoons (100 ml) heavy cream

3 coffee beans

⅓ cup (60 g) superfine granulated sugar

1 oz (30 g) flan or pastry cream powder (or
    cornstarch)

6 teaspoons (10 g) unsweetened
    cocoa powder

1 whole egg (1½ oz/50 g)

4 egg yolks (about 3 oz/80 g)

For the choux paste

½ cup + 2 tablespoons (150 ml) water

7 tablespoons (100 ml) whole milk

1 heaping teaspoon (5 g) superfine
    granulated sugar

5 pinches table salt

7 tablespoons (100 g) unsalted butter

1 cup + 3 tablespoons (150 g) cake flour

5 whole eggs (about 8½ oz/250 g)

For the glaze

1 egg

1 tablespoon milk

1 pinch table salt

KITCHEN UTENSILS

Whisk; electronic thermometer; 2 piping
bags with 2 round tips, No. 6 and No. 12
(¼ in and ½ in) respectively; pastry brush;
decorating spatula; pastry comb (or fine-
pronged fork); plastic wrap; parchment
paper; fine-mesh strainer

A **word** from **Gilles** Marchal

This recipe is the epitome of French *pâtisserie* and a particular specialty at La Maison du Chocolat. Flan or pastry cream powder is a mixture of starches (including cornstarch) flavored with vanilla. But you can use the same quantity of wheat or rice flour, or even cornstarch, instead.

The icing and pastry cream can be prepared the night before, but I recommend making the choux pastry the day you plan to serve the éclairs. The icing will keep quite well in the refrigerator for several days. It also makes an ideal topping for a small cake or madeleine—and even a lovely chocolate sauce to pour over profiteroles.

DIRECTIONS

For the icing
▣ Soften the gelatine sheets in very cold water for 15 minutes.

▣ In a 6½-in (16-cm) saucepan, combine the water, sugar, cocoa, and heavy cream. Heat the mixture to approximately 216°F/102°C, stirring regularly, to obtain a perfect icing that will set well on the choux pastry. To make sure the mixture has the right texture, dip the back of a teaspoon into the icing. The spoon should be coated with a thick enough layer of icing that it does not show through.

▣ Remove from the heat, add the gelatine sheets (after squeezing out the excess water) and mix. Leave to cool slightly.

For the pastry cream
▣ Finely chop the chocolate with a large knife and set aside in a mixing bowl. In a saucepan, bring the milk to a boil with the heavy cream and the coffee beans. In another mixing bowl, mix the sugar, flan powder, and cocoa; add the egg and the yolks, beating them until they turn a pale yellow color. Remove the coffee beans from the milk. Pour the egg mixture into a boiling liquid and leave it over the heat as you

beat it vigorously. Bring the pastry cream to a boil and cook for 1 minute. Once it has thickened, remove it from the heat and pour it over the chocolate. Leave to melt for 2 minutes, then whisk vigorously until well blended.

▣ Pour the chocolate cream into a very clean mixing bowl and cover it with plastic wrap. Cool as quickly as possible by setting the pastry cream in the freezer for 1 hour, then leave to chill in the refrigerator (up to 48 hours maximum). This pastry cream is very fragile and sensitive to changes in temperature, so be sure to remove it from room temperature as quickly as possible. Before using, mix the pastry cream gently to soften it.

For the choux paste
▣ Preheat the oven to 465°F/240°C.

▣ In a saucepan, bring the water to a boil with the milk, sugar, salt, and butter. Add the sifted flour, and using a spatula, stir vigorously; the mixture should form a relatively firm paste. Continue to cook for 1 to 2 minutes to dry out the paste. Remove from the heat and add the eggs one by one, mixing to obtain a soft, smooth, and glossy dough.

▣ For the glaze, beat the egg, milk, and salt together and strain.

▣ Fill a piping bag, fitted with the No. 12 (½ in) tip, with choux paste. Cover a baking sheet with parchment paper, then form 5½ in (14 cm) éclairs spaced at least 1 in (3 cm) apart.

▣ Using a pastry brush, baste the tops with the glaze, then create subtle lines by running the pastry comb along the tops lengthwise.

▣ Place in the oven. Turn off the heat, and wait until the éclairs have puffed up but are not yet browned before opening the oven door slightly (⅜ in or 1 cm) for 1 minute to release the steam that would otherwise prevent the choux paste from drying out. Bring the oven temperature back to 340°F/170°C. Bake the éclairs for approximately 30 minutes, until nicely browned.

Finishing touches
▣ Let the éclairs cool, then pierce three holes into the top of each to fill them with the chocolate pastry cream using the No. 6 (¼ in) tip. Warm the icing to 95°F/35°C.

▣ Using a spatula, coat the top of each éclair (or carefully dip them in the icing top down). Remove any excess icing with your index finger. Place the éclairs in the refrigerator. Remove them 15 minutes before serving.

Dark Chocolate Shortbread Tart

Makes 6 tartlets

Preparation time: **20 minutes**

Resting time: **2 hours**

Cooking time: **25 minutes**

FROM THE STORES

For the shortbread

½ Tahitian vanilla bean

10 tablespoons (140 g) unsalted butter

2 tablespoons (10 g) ground almonds

2 generous pinches table salt

½ cup (60 g) confectioners' sugar

1 egg (1¾ oz/50 g)

1½ cups (200 g) cake flour

For the dark chocolate ganache

7½ oz (200 g) dark chocolate 60% cocoa

¾ cup (200 ml) heavy cream

2 tablespoons (30 g) unsalted butter

KITCHEN UTENSILS

6 individual tart molds, 4 in (10 cm) in diameter
(preferably metal)

Pastry cutter slightly larger in diameter than
the tart molds

Rolling pin

DIRECTIONS

For the shortbread

◙ Split the bean down its length and scrape out the seeds from the inside using the tip of a knife. In a mixing bowl, cream the butter until softened. Add the ground almonds, salt, confectioners' sugar, and the vanilla seeds. Work the dough slightly until it becomes grainy, then add the egg and the sifted flour. Mix well to obtain a dough with an even consistency.

◙ Place the ball of dough on a sheet of parchment paper, cover it with a second sheet, then roll it out to a very even ³⁄₁₆-in (5-mm) thickness. Remove the top sheet of paper, then use the pastry cutter to cut out 6 rounds of dough. Arrange them in the molds, cut off the excess dough, and press lightly so that the dough lines the inside of the molds. Refrigerate for another 2 hours.

◙ Preheat the oven to 150°C/300°F. Prick the tart crusts several times with a fork, then bake for 20 to 25 minutes; after baking, the dough should be an even golden brown color, both top and bottom.

For the dark chocolate ganache

◙ Finely chop the chocolate and set aside in a mixing bowl. In a saucepan, bring the heavy cream to a boil. Pour it over the chocolate, covering the chocolate completely. Leave the chocolate to melt for 2 minutes without touching it, then whisk lightly in small circles, starting from the center.

◙ When the ganache thickens, move the whisk toward the sides of the bowl until you obtain a smooth texture. Gradually add the butter, in small bits, and continue to mix gently, to obtain a silky, glossy ganache. Divide the ganache, which should still be warm and liquid, among the tart crusts. Leave these delights in the refrigerator for 1 hour before enjoying them.

A **word** from **Gilles** Marchal

This chocolate tart is renowned the world over. At La Maison du Chocolat, we have been following the same recipe scrupulously for thirty years, preparing it exactly the same way every morning in Paris, London, Tokyo, New York, and Hong Kong. I like to serve it with a soft, spiced caramel, a fruit compote, or a citrus zest praline. The shortbread can be prepared the day before by filling the tart molds with dough and then leaving them in the refrigerator. The way the crust is baked is essential to the flavor and how well the dessert lasts. Personally, I prefer it slightly crisp rather than underdone.

Orange Blossom Éclairs with Wild Strawberries

Makes 15 éclairs
Preparation time: **2 hours**
Resting time: **2 hours**
Cooking time: **40 minutes**

For the pastry cream

1⅔ cups (400 ml) whole milk
7 tablespoons (100 ml) heavy cream
1 Bourbon vanilla bean
⅓ cup (70 g) superfine granulated sugar
1 oz (30 g) flan or pastry cream powder
1 whole egg
4 egg yolks (3 oz/80 g)
2 tablespoons orange blossom water

For the choux paste

½ cup + 2 tablespoons (150 ml) water
7 tablespoons (100 ml) milk
2 heaping teaspoons (10 g) superfine
   granulated sugar
5 pinches table salt
7 tablespoons (100 g) unsalted butter
1 cup + 3 tablespoons (150 g) cake flour
5 whole eggs (about 8½ oz/250 g)

For the glaze

1 egg
1 tablespoon whole milk
1 pinch table salt

For the decoration

4 oz (150 g) milk chocolate 35% to
   40% cocoa
2 pints wild strawberries
Several drops of honey

KITCHEN UTENSILS

Electronic thermometer; 2 piping bags
with 2 round tips, No. 8 and No. 12 (⁵⁄₁₆ in
and ½ in) respectively; pastry comb (or
fine-pronged fork); parchment paper;
whisk; 12 × 2 in (30 × 5 cm) acetate or
plastic sheet; ruler; spatula

A **word** from **Gilles** Marchal

Choux paste is extremely simple to make—as long as you take your time. I suggest you prepare the pastry cream and the chocolate topping the night before, to make things easier the following day. *Petites Fleurs* strawberries are a wild variety with a subtle taste. You can also substitute Mara des Bois strawberries or even raspberries.

Try replacing the thin layer of chocolate with milk chocolate shavings made using a paring knife and arranged on top of the cream along the éclair.

DIRECTIONS

For the pastry cream

◉ In a saucepan, bring the milk and heavy cream to a boil with the vanilla bean (split lengthwise and seeded). In a mixing bowl, combine the superfine granulated sugar and pastry cream powder. Add the egg and the egg yolks. Stir until the mixture begins to turn pale yellow. Pour the mixture into a boiling, vanilla-flavored milk, beating vigorously. Bring the cream to a boil and leave on the heat for 1 minute. Once the cream has thickened, remove the vanilla bean and pour the cream into a mixing bowl. Leave to cool slightly. Cover with plastic wrap and set aside for 2 hours in the refrigerator.

For the choux paste

◉ Preheat the oven to 465°F/240°C.
◉ In a saucepan, bring the water to a boil with the milk, sugar, salt, and butter. Add the sifted flour, and using a spatula, stir vigorously; the mixture should form a relatively firm paste. Continue to cook for 1 to 2 minutes to dry out the paste. Remove from heat and add the eggs one by one, mixing to obtain a soft, smooth, and glossy dough.
◉ For the glaze, beat the egg, milk, and salt together and strain.

◉ Fill the piping bag, fitted with the No. 12 (½ in) tip, with choux paste. Cover a baking sheet with parchment paper, then form 5½ in (14 cm) éclairs spaced at least 1 in (3 cm) apart.
◉ Using a pastry brush, baste the tops with the glaze, then create subtle lines by running the pastry comb along the tops lengthwise.
◉ Place in the oven. Turn off the heat, and wait until the éclairs have puffed up but are not yet browned before opening the oven door slightly (⅜ in or 1 cm) for 1 minute to release the steam that would otherwise prevent the choux paste from drying out. Bring the oven temperature back to 340°F/170°C. Bake the éclairs for approximately 30 minutes, until nicely browned.

For the decoration

◉ Chop the milk chocolate and melt it slowly in a bain-marie, stirring regularly, until it reaches a maximum temperature of 84–86°F/29–30°C. Take care not to exceed this temperature. Pour the melted chocolate onto the sheet of acetate, spreading it out to a uniform thickness of approximately 1/32 in (1 to 1½ mm). Let the chocolate set, but before it hardens, use a ruler to cut it into 5½-×-1-in (14-×-2-cm) strips. Chill for 30 minutes.

◉ Remove the chocolate strips from the acetate and return to the refrigerator.

Presentation

◉ Using a serrated knife, form a ⅜-in (1-cm) wide groove lengthwise along the top of the éclairs. Whisk the orange blossom water and the vanilla-flavored pastry cream together. Using the piping bag fitted with the No. 8 (5/16 in) tip, fill the éclairs with the pastry cream alternating with a few wild strawberries. Let the pastry cream spill over the top of the éclairs slightly to prevent the thin strips of milk chocolate from sliding. Decorate with a beautiful wild strawberry and several drops of honey.
◉ These treats were made to be enjoyed at any time of day.

Gift-Wrapped Chocolate Zabaglione and Hazelnut Gems

Serves 12
Preparation time: **2 hours**
Resting time: **2 hours**
Cooking time: **20 minutes**

FROM THE **STORES**

For the biscuit

3 eggs
⅓ cup packed (80 g) almond paste
   (50% almonds)
1¾ oz (50 g) dark chocolate 70% cocoa
2 teaspoons (10 g) unsweetened cocoa
   powder
⅓ cup (60 g) superfine granulated sugar

For the hazelnut gems

½ cup + 2 tablespoons (120 g) superfine
   granulated sugar
7 tablespoons (100 ml) water
1 Bourbon vanilla bean
9 oz (250 g) shelled Piedmont hazelnuts

For the cream

1 cup (250 ml) heavy cream
1 Bourbon vanilla bean
¼ star anise pod
1 green cardamom pod
20 whole coriander seeds
1 small stick cinnamon
3 twists of the black pepper mill
⅓ cup (70 g) superfine granulated sugar

For the chocolate zabaglione

1¼ cups (300 ml) heavy cream
1 whole egg (about 1 oz/50 g)
4 egg yolks (about 3 oz/80 g)
½ cup (90 g) superfine granulated sugar
2 tablespoons (30 ml) water
6½ oz (180 g) dark chocolate 70% cocoa

KITCHEN UTENSILS

Electronic thermometer, piping bag with No.
10 (⅜ in) round tip, electric mixer, 12 small
gift boxes with lid and ribbon, rubber spatula,
silicone spatula, parchment paper, fine-
mesh strainer

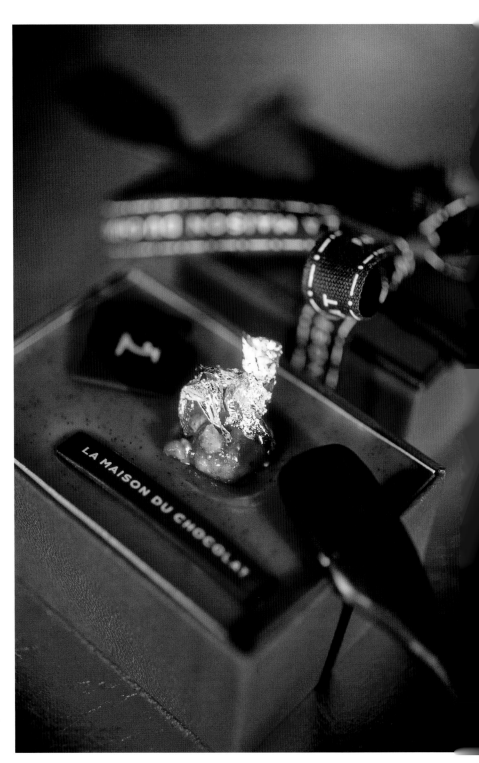

A word from Gilles Marchal

Serving this dessert is a true gift to your friends and family. Keep the chocolate boxes from La Maison du Chocolat on hand to prepare it. This zabaglione will add a flourish to a family meal, or it can be served to friends with a rich vanilla or caramel ice cream.

DIRECTIONS

For the biscuit

◉ Separate the egg whites and yolks. Break the almond paste into small pieces. Using the mixer, beat the egg yolks with the almond paste until the mixture turns a pale yellow color. Set aside. Chop up the chocolate and melt in a bain-marie. Add the cocoa.

◉ Preheat the oven to 410°F/210°C. Beat the egg whites until they form stiff peaks, gradually pouring in the sugar while beating. Fold the whites into the almond paste mixture, then pour the mixture over the melted chocolate. Stir very gently with a rubber spatula. Cover a baking sheet with parchment paper, and then use the silicone spatula to spread out the biscuit batter over a 10-×-10-in (25-×-25-cm) surface. Bake for 7 to 8 minutes; your biscuit should remain soft. Leave to cool. Cut into pieces slightly smaller than the inside of the gift boxes. Place in the refrigerator.

For the hazelnut gems

◉ In a saucepan approximately 20 cm (8 in) in diameter, cook the sugar with the water and the vanilla bean, split in half lengthwise, seeds scraped, until the temperature reaches 250°F/120°C. Add the hazelnuts. Stir them with a silicone spatula to coat them evenly with a thin layer of sugar and caramelize them completely.

◉ Spread out the hazelnuts on a sheet of parchment paper, setting aside two dozen for decoration. Leave the rest to cool before crushing them into large pieces. Set aside in an airtight container in a dry place.

For the cream

◉ In a saucepan, bring the heavy cream to a boil with the vanilla bean (split in half lengthwise, seeds scraped), star anise pod, cardamom pod (crushed), coriander seeds, cinnamon, and black pepper. Remove from the heat, cover, and steep until cool. Put the saucepan back on the heat and bring to a boil. Strain to remove the spices. You will reheat the cream just before pouring it over the sugar in the next step.

◉ In a saucepan with a 6-in (16-cm) diameter, cook the sugar dry just until it begins to smoke, stirring constantly, to obtain a relatively dark caramel. Remove from the heat and pour in the hot, spiced cream while beating vigorously; the caramel should become smooth and glossy. Set aside in an airtight container.

For the chocolate zabaglione

◉ In an electric mixer, whip the cream, stopping before it becomes too firm, and set aside in the refrigerator. In a bowl, beat the egg and the yolks in an electric mixer until they turn a pale yellow. In a saucepan, cook the sugar with the water until the temperature reaches 250°F/120°C. Carefully pour the syrup over the beaten eggs.

Whip to obtain a frothy, slightly firm mixture. Break up the chocolate and melt in a bain-marie to 115°F/45°C. Gently mix the cooled zabaglione with the whipped cream. Fold approximately one-third of this mixture into the chocolate using a rubber spatula, beat vigorously, then add the second and third portions, mixing with the spatula after each addition.

Presentation

◉ Line the insides of the boxes with parchment paper (or, better yet, with a thin sheet of edible gold leaf). Place the biscuit in the bottom, and sprinkle generously with crushed hazelnuts. Using the piping bag with the No. 10 (⅜ in) tip, fill the boxes three-quarters full with the chocolate zabaglione. Refrigerate for 2 hours. Warm the caramel to 95 to 105°F/35 to 40°C, then spread it over the entire surface of the zabaglione to a depth of ¹⁄₁₆ in (2 mm). Arrange an attractive caramelized hazelnut on top like a jewel, and decorate with chocolate and gold leaf as desired. Put the lid on the box and tie an attractive knot. Place the boxes in the refrigerator, removing them 15 minutes before dessert time.

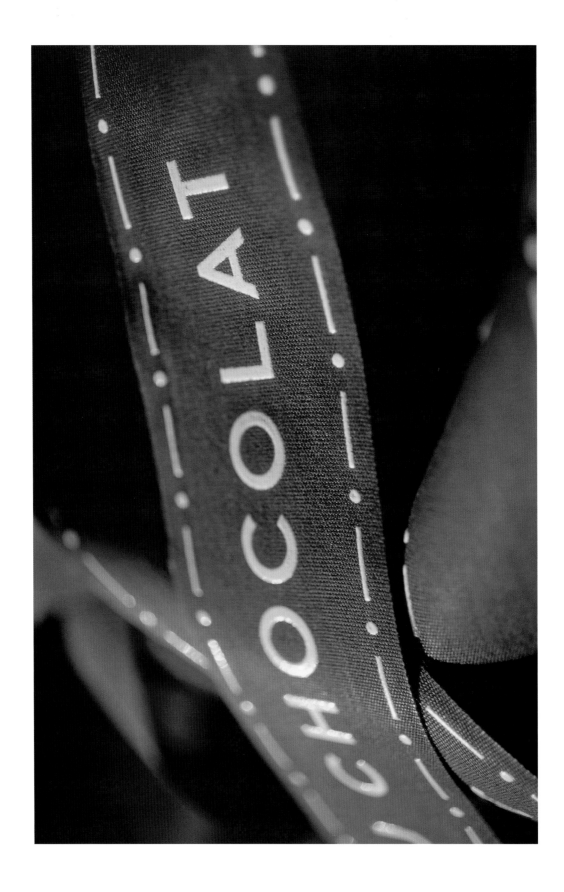

Charlottes with Chocolate and Passion Fruit Mousse

Makes 6 individual charlottes

Preparation time: **2 hours**

Resting time: **2 hours**

Cooking time: **1 hour**

FROM THE STORES

For the ladyfingers

3 eggs (3 oz/90 g of whites and
    2 oz/60 g of yolks)

½ cup + 2 tablespoons (75 g) cake flour

1 tablespoon (10 g) potato starch

⅓ cup (75 g) superfine granulated sugar

1 pinch table salt

½ cup (50 g) confectioners' sugar

For the chocolate–passion fruit mousse

5 oz (150 g) dark chocolate 65% cocoa

4 teaspoons (20 ml) passion fruit juice

½ Maracuja passion fruit

1 cup (300 ml) heavy cream

For the cocoa-cream icing

½ cup (120 ml) water

¾ cup (150 g) superfine granulated sugar

¾ cup (60 g) unsweetened cocoa powder

7 tablespoons (100 ml) heavy cream

4 sheets gelatine (about ⅓ oz/8 g)

Presentation

3 oz (80 g) dark chocolate 60% cocoa

2 cups (½ liter) passion fruit sorbet

1 Maracuja passion fruit

KITCHEN UTENSILS

Electric mixer

Electronic thermometer

Whisk

Paring knife

Piping bag with No. 8 (⁵⁄₁₆ in) round tip

Cheesecloth or fine-mesh, conical strainer

Rubber spatula

Parchment paper

There are two different methods for preparing this recipe. The first method is quicker (charlotte in a glass), while the other (as shown in the photo) is served in tubes for a truly spectacular dessert.

To serve in glasses

6 attractive glasses

To serve in tubes

5 in (12 cm) square plastic box

Wooden skewers

6 stainless steel or plastic tubes, 5 in (12 cm)
    long and 1¼ in (3 cm) wide, available in
    specialty cake-making stores

Plastic wrap

Sheets of flexible acetate (5 × 2½ in/
    12 × 6 cm)

If you can't find tubes, making them yourself is simple: cut unused PVC tubes into 5-in (12-cm) pieces. Line the inside with flexible acetate and close off one end using plastic wrap. Place the tubes in the plastic box, making sure that they stay completely upright.

DIRECTIONS

For the ladyfingers

◉ Preheat the oven to 410°F/210°C. Separate the egg whites and yolks. In a mixing bowl, sift together the flour and potato starch. In another mixing bowl, beat the egg yolks with 2 tablespoons (25 g) of the superfine granulated sugar until the mixture turns a pale yellow color.

◉ Beat the egg whites with a pinch of salt until they form stiff peaks; just before they become firm, gradually pour in the remainder of the sugar in several additions. Pour the sugar–egg yolk mixture over the whites, stirring in with a wooden spoon. Add the sifted flour and potato starch, then stir the batter as gently as possible.

◉ Cover a baking sheet with parchment paper, then use the piping bag with a round tip to make small rectangles of batter approximately 2½ in (6 to 7 cm) long: you will need 5 for each charlotte. Using the strainer, sprinkle confectioners' sugar over the ladyfingers before placing them in the oven. Bake for 4 to 5 minutes. Leave to cool, then cut the fingers in half widthwise. Set aside in a dry place.

A **word** from **Gilles** Marchal

You can prepare this dessert entirely the night before: you just need to ice the charlottes a few hours before dessert time. When I was an apprentice with Claude Bourguignon, I used to make a fabulous recipe for Sachertorte, a classic Austrian dessert. I replaced the syrup with passion fruit juice. To make a more Sachertorte-style dessert, try dusting the mousse with cocoa.

If you're short on time, you can buy ready-made ladyfingers. If you do, remove the excess confectioners' sugar and cut the ladyfingers into small batons.

For the chocolate–passion fruit mousse

▣ Chop up the dark chocolate and melt it in a bain-marie.

▣ Whip 4 teaspoons (180 ml) of very cold heavy cream to obtain the same texture as whipped cream, but less firm. Set aside in the refrigerator.

▣ In a saucepan, bring the remainder of the heavy cream to a boil. Pour it over the chocolate. Let stand for 2 minutes, add the juice and seeds from the passion fruit (removed from their rind using a teaspoon), then whisk vigorously, starting in the center and working outwards to obtain a smooth, glossy ganache. Add the whipped cream in three phases: mix in the first portion vigorously with the whisk, then fold in the two remaining portions delicately with the rubber spatula. If you decide to serve in tubes, use the piping bag to fill each tube with chocolate mousse. Freeze for 3 hours. If you are serving in glasses, fill the bottom of each glass with a small quantity of mousse and then "plant" the sponge fingers in the mousse, sticking them to the wall of the glass. Leave the glasses to chill in the refrigerator for 3 hours.

For the cocoa-cream icing

▣ Soften the gelatine sheets in very cold water.

▣ In a 6½-in (16-cm) saucepan, combine the water, sugar, cocoa, and heavy cream. Stir constantly. Heat the mixture to a temperature of 215 to 217°F/102 to 103°C. Remove from heat, add the gelatine sheets (after wringing out excess water), and mix. Leave to cool slightly. Cover the ladyfingers with the icing when it is at 100 to 104°F/38 to 40°C.

Presentation

In glasses

▣ Once the mousse has set, cover the entire surface with icing. Leave to harden for 2 minutes. Decorate with dark chocolate shavings. Place the glasses in the refrigerator for 1 hour, removing them 15 minutes before serving for the final touch.

In tubes

▣ Once the mousse is quite firm, remove the tubes and the acetate. Place the mousses on a rack and cover them completely with icing. Leave to harden for 2 minutes.

▣ Stand 1 tube of chocolate mousse in the center of each plate, using 2 wooden skewers stuck into each end for support.

▣ Stick the sponge finger halves vertically on to one side of the tubes (see photo). Decorate the ends of the tubes with dark chocolate shavings made using a paring knife, or with a thin chocolate round. Leave in the refrigerator for 1 hour, removing them 15 minutes before serving.

▣ Arrange several passion fruit seeds and some fresh juice around each charlotte. Top with a small scoop of sorbet. Enjoy immediately.

Charlottes with Chocolate and Passion Fruit Mousse

Mother's Homemade Chocolate Mousse

Serves 4–6
Preparation time: **20 minutes**
Resting time: **2 hours**
No cooking required

FROM THE **STORES**

For the mousse

4 eggs (about 7½ oz/200 g)
6½ oz (180 g) dark chocolate 55% cocoa
3 tablespoons (40 g) unsalted butter
1 tablespoon unsweetened cocoa powder
⅓ cup (60 g) superfine granulated sugar
1 tablespoon Lorraine Mirabelle plum liqueur
1 pinch salt

Presentation

1 bar dark chocolate 60% cocoa

KITCHEN UTENSILS

Electric mixer

Paring knife or small utility knife

DIRECTIONS

For the mousse

▣ Separate the egg whites and yolks. Break the chocolate into pieces and melt in a bain-marie with the butter and cocoa. Remove from the heat, whisk the egg yolks one by one, whisking vigorously, and add the sugar.

▣ In an electric mixer, beat the egg whites with a pinch of salt until they form stiff peaks, then fold them carefully into the egg yolk mixture. Add the liqueur. Pour the mousse into an attractive bowl (glass is best), then refrigerate for 2 hours.

Presentation

▣ Using a paring knife or other small knife, shave the chocolate directly onto the mousse, covering the entire surface. For children, shave milk chocolate rather than dark chocolate over the mousse.

A **word** from **Gilles** Marchal

I have given you the actual recipe from my childhood, which my mother always makes. This mousse is a surprisingly simple dish. If you take the time to create delicious little pleasures like this more often, they will never leave your side. For those of you who like coffee, try adding a few roasted and crushed coffee beans to the mousse. You can also replace the subtle taste of Lorraine Mirabelle in this mousse with aged, dark amber rum.

Above: Lake of dark gold
Opposite: Some overflow

Black and White Cookies

Makes 20 cookies

Preparation time: **1 hour**

Resting time: **1 hour**

Cooking time: **20 minutes**

FROM THE STORES

3½ oz (100 g) dark chocolate 60% cocoa

1¾ oz (50 g) milk chocolate 35% to 40% cocoa

1¾ oz (50 g) white "chocolate"

11 tablespoons (150 g) unsalted butter

¾ cup + 1 tablespoon packed (180 g) + ¼ cup packed (50 g) brown sugar

3 pinches salt

½ vanilla bean

1½ cups + 1 tablespoon (200 g) cake flour

1 teaspoon (3 to 4 g) dry yeast

1 egg (1¾ oz/50 g)

KITCHEN UTENSILS

Cheesecloth or fine-mesh strainer

Parchment paper

DIRECTIONS

▣ Finely chop the chocolates and set aside in a mixing bowl. In another mixing bowl, soften the butter slightly. Add both types of sugar and the salt. Split the vanilla bean in half lengthwise and scrape the seeds out over the bowl. Mix slightly. Sift the flour and the yeast over the mixture and add the egg; continue to mix to obtain a dough with an even consistency. Add the chopped chocolate. Form the dough into a large cylinder, approximately 2½ in (60 cm) in diameter. Chill for 1 hour in the refrigerator, then cut into ½-in (1½-cm) rounds.

▣ Preheat the oven to 355°F/180°C.

▣ Cover a baking sheet with parchment paper, then arrange the rounds of dough on the sheet, spaced 1½ in (3 to 4 cm) apart. Flatten slightly with the palm of your hand. Bake for approximately 20 minutes; the cookies should remain soft in the center.

▣ Leave to cool before eating. These cookies will keep very well for several days in an airtight container stored in a dry place.

A **word** from **Gilles** Marchal

Cookies are the quintessential North American pastry. In the United States, cooks add pieces of hazelnuts, almonds, pecans, or dried fruit. There are even savory cookies. Canadians like to replace some of the butter with peanut butter and flavor their cookies with maple syrup.

You can make your cookies with just milk chocolate or dark chocolate.

Double Chocolate Macarons

Makes 10 large or 50 small macarons

Preparation time: **1 hour 15 minutes**

Resting time: **1 hour**

Cooking time: **20 minutes**

FROM THE STORES

For the ganache

1¾ oz (150 g) dark chocolate 65% cocoa

½ cup + 2 tablespoons (150 ml) heavy cream

4 tablespoons (50 g) unsalted butter

For the macarons

1⅔ cup (200 g) confectioners' sugar

3 tablespoons (15 g) unsweetened cocoa
  powder

1¼ cups (120 g) ground almonds

¾ cup (160 g) superfine granulated sugar

3 tablespoons (50 ml) mineral water

4 egg whites (about 4 oz/120 g)

1 pinch table salt

KITCHEN UTENSILS

Fine-mesh strainer

Piping bag with No. 10 or No. 8 (⅜ in or
  ⁵⁄₁₆ in) tip

Electronic thermometer

Whisk

Electric mixer

Parchment paper

DIRECTIONS

For the ganache

◙ Finely chop the chocolate and set aside in a mixing bowl. In a saucepan, bring the heavy cream to a boil. Pour it over the chocolate. Leave the chocolate to melt for 2 minutes, then whisk lightly in small circles, starting from the center. When the ganache thickens, move the whisk toward the sides of the bowl until you obtain a smooth texture. Gradually add the butter, in small bits, and continue to stir gently to obtain a silky, glossy ganache. Set aside at room temperature while preparing the macarons. You will end up with a ganache the consistency of pastry cream, perfect for filling the macarons.

For the macarons

◙ Preheat the oven to 300°F/150°C and cover a baking sheet with parchment paper. In a mixing bowl, using the fine-mesh strainer, sift together the confectioners' sugar, cocoa, and ground almonds. In a saucepan, cook the superfine granulated sugar with the water to obtain a syrup. Once the temperature reaches approximately 220°F/105°C, begin beating two of the egg whites with a pinch of salt until they form very stiff peaks, while continuing to let the syrup cook. When the syrup reaches precisely 244°F/118°C, immediately pour the sugar syrup carefully over the stiff egg whites, continuing to beat until you have a firm meringue.

Add the sifted dry ingredients, then add the remaining egg whites while mixing. Continue to mix until the macaron batter is smooth; it should be glossy and form ribbons. Fill your piping bag with batter, using the No. 10 (⅜ in) tip for large macarons or the No. 8 (⁵⁄₁₆ in) tip for small macarons.

◙ Form balls on the baking sheet, 2 in (5 cm) in diameter for large macarons or ¾ in (2 cm) for small ones. Bake large macarons for approximately 12 minutes, small for approximately 9 minutes: they should form a thin, crunchy shell on the top and sides, but remain soft in the center.

◙ Leave to cool before flipping over. Spread chocolate ganache over half of the macaron shells. Top with the non-iced halves to form sandwiches.

A **word** from
Gilles Marchal

The macaron is a symbol of culture and refinement in French *pâtisserie*. Originating from the cities of Nancy and Boulay in northeastern France, macarons are now world renowned with one famous example being the Italian cakes flavored with Amaretto (sweet almond liqueur). My own favorites are the recipe my great-uncle Antoine Beck used to make at the Place du Clocher in Saint-Émilion and, of course, La Maison du Chocolat's superb macarons. They are unique in that each one is filled with ganache. From Paris to New York, London to Tokyo, and Cannes to Hong Kong, macarons have become one of La Maison du Chocolat's biggest successes.

Try sprinkling the unbaked balls of macaron dough with dried, unsweetened coconut or cocoa nibs, and flavoring your chocolate ganache with bergamot zest, fresh herbs, vanilla, or your favorite spice.

Chocolate Meeting **Coffee** over a **Tiramisu**

Serves 6

Preparation time: **1 hour 30 minutes**

Resting time: **2 hours**

Cooking time: **30 minutes**

For the chocolate-coffee cream

4½ oz (120 g) dark chocolate

¾ cup (200 ml) whole milk

4 teaspoons (20 g) ground Colombian coffee

5 teaspoons packed (25 g) brown sugar

7 tablespoons (100 ml) heavy cream

1 whole egg

1 egg yolk

6 large ladyfingers (see recipe page 56)

½ cup + 2 tablespoons (150 ml) brewed
espresso

For the mascarpone cream

½ cup + 2 tablespoons (150 ml) heavy cream,
cold

3 egg yolks (2 oz/60 g)

6 tablespoons (80 g) superfine granulated
sugar

10½ oz (300 g) mascarpone

2 tablespoons (30 ml) almond liqueur

Presentation

Milk chocolate shavings

Unsweetened cocoa powder

KITCHEN UTENSILS

Electronic thermometer

Whisk

6 clear glasses

Cheesecloth or fine-mesh strainer

Pastry brush

Rubber spatula

DIRECTIONS

For the chocolate-coffee cream

◙ Finely chop the chocolate and set aside in a mixing bowl. In a saucepan, bring the milk to a boil. Add the ground coffee and the sugar. Remove from the heat, cover, and leave to steep until cool. Strain the liquid.

◙ Pour the flavored milk into the saucepan and bring back to a boil, adding the heavy cream and then the egg and egg yolk. Cook as you would a custard to reach a temperature of 181°F/83°C. Strain directly over the chocolate. Leave to melt for 2 minutes, then whisk gently, working from the center outwards to obtain a smooth, velvety cream.

◙ Pour the warm cream into the bottoms of 6 glasses. Arrange one or more ladyfingers in the center of the chocolate-coffee cream, without allowing them to touch the sides of the glass. Use the pastry brush to baste them generously with espresso. You can also dip the ladyfingers in the espresso before arranging them in the cream. Refrigerate for 2 hours.

For the mascarpone cream

◙ Whisk the cold heavy cream into a firm whipped cream. Place in the refrigerator.

◙ In a container set over a bain-marie, beat the eggs and sugar to cook them like a zabaglione: they should be foamy and warm (approximately 175°F/80°C). Mix the almond liqueur into the mascarpone using a rubber spatula. Add the cooked egg yolk–sugar mixture, then the whipped cream. Fill the glasses with the mascarpone cream. Set them in the refrigerator for 2 hours.

◙ Just before serving, sprinkle each tiramisu with a few milk chocolate shavings (created using a paring knife) and powder with cocoa. Enjoy chilled.

A **word** from **Gilles** Marchal

If you like traditional tiramisu, you'll love this reinterpretation with its subtle hint of chocolate-coffee cream and touch of milk chocolate. For a different treat, try creating your own recipe by replacing the ground coffee infusion in the chocolate cream with cinnamon or a fresh herb, or by adding a thin layer of homemade jam (apricot or blackberry would be perfect).

Chocolate Cake with Dark Gold Nuggets

Makes 1 cake

(6 servings)

Preparation time: **45 minutes**

Cooking time: **50 minutes**

FROM THE STORES

For the cake batter

3 oz (80 g) dark chocolate 65% cocoa

4 tablespoons (60 g) unsalted butter

½ orange

1 cup (120 g) flour

½ oz (20 g) unsweetened cocoa powder

1 heaping teaspoon (5 g) dry yeast

6 egg yolks (4 oz/120 g)

¾ cup (150 g) superfine granulated sugar

⅓ cup (90 g) heavy cream

For the orange glaze

1⅔ cup (200 g) confectioners' sugar

3 tablespoons (40 ml) orange juice

3 teaspoons (20 g) honey

1 tablespoon orange blossom water

KITCHEN UTENSILS

Cake tin, 8 in (20 cm) long and 3 in (7 to 8 cm)
    wide

Microplane grater

Fine-mesh strainer

Pastry brush

Cooling rack

Parchment paper

DIRECTIONS

For the cake batter

◙ Preheat the oven to 300°F/150°C.

◙ Finely chop the dark chocolate. Melt the butter in a bain-marie. Zest the orange.

◙ In a mixing bowl, sift together the flour, the cocoa, and the yeast. In another mixing bowl, gently beat the egg yolks with the sugar. Add the orange zest and cream, then the sifted dry ingredients, the warm melted butter, and finally the chopped chocolate. Mix together thoroughly.

◙ Grease the cake tin lightly and line with parchment paper. Fill with batter to four-fifths of the tin's height. Bake for approximately 50 minutes (check by pricking the cake with a knife tip: if it comes out clean, the cake is done). Leave the cake to cool in the pan on a cooling rack before unmolding.

For the orange glaze

◙ Sift the confectioners' sugar.

◙ In a saucepan, warm half the orange juice and orange blossom water with the honey. Leave to cool, then add the remaining juice, water, and the sugar.

◙ You can prepare your glaze in advance and store it in an airtight container.

Presentation

◙ Preheat the oven to 220°C/425°F. Using a pastry brush, glaze the top and sides of the cake. Place on a baking sheet and put in the oven for 30 to 40 seconds, just long enough to crystallize the sugar in the glaze. Leave to cool.

◙ This cake will keep very well for 2 days covered in plastic wrap.

A **word** from **Gilles** Marchal

It's a real pleasure to make cake from recipes that have been passed down through the generations in your own kitchen. Every chef has his or her own recipes and preferences. My favorite part about baking these homemade cakes is the mouth-watering fragrances that waft out from the kitchen.

Playful
Uses
for
Chocolate

Camille Hammerer and Vanessa Batut

Camille and Vanessa have been working together for over three years. They love to sculpt materials to bring them to life. Scraps of fabric, elements from nature, flea-market finds, beautiful color combinations, collections of ribbon—all of these can be the inspiration for creating works that exude sensitivity, humanity, and sensuality. For La Maison du Chocolat, they chose to create an Ode to Chocolate, the supreme temptation.

Their luscious sculpture is composed of the ingredients of chocolate and its manufacturing process. Pods, beans, nibs, cocoa butter, molds, unrefined bars, and refined chocolates, embellished with gilded fruit and tempting macarons made of leather, and all feeding the carnal desire to give in to temptation.

Suspended **Cocoa Fettuccine,** Italian Style

Serves 6

Preparation time: **2 hours**

Resting time: **30 minutes**

Cooking time: **15 minutes**

FROM THE **STORES**

For the fettuccine

2½ cups (350 g) cake flour

½ cup (50 g) finely ground hazelnuts

¼ cup (20 g) unsweetened cocoa powder

3 clementines

2 eggs (about 3½ oz/100 g)

For the chocolate cream

3½ oz (100 g) milk chocolate 35% to 40% cocoa

1¾ oz (50 g) dark chocolate 70% cocoa

¾ cup (200 ml) whole milk

7 tablespoons (100 ml) heavy cream

3 egg yolks (2 oz/60 g)

For the reduced clementine juice

9 clementines

¼ cup (50 g) superfine granulated sugar

3 tablespoons (50 ml) Grand Marnier®

Presentation

1 bar white "chocolate"

3 quarts water

2 fresh bay leaves

KITCHEN UTENSILS

Colander

Fine-mesh strainer

Electronic thermometer

Pasta machine or rolling pin

Microplane grater

Lemon juicer

1½-in (4-cm) stainless steel, round pastry cutter

Wooden spoons with long, round handles

Rubber spatula

Large tray

Whisk

A **word** from **Gilles** Marchal

This dessert is sure to surprise your friends. I also love serving the fettuccine with flambéed Grand Marnier® poured over the pasta. During hunting season, this cocoa-flavored fettuccine is also the perfect complement to venison, hare, or any other game. Stray off the beaten track and try making this unique pasta yourself. Is it a main dish or a dessert? The choice is yours!

DIRECTIONS

For the fettuccine

▣ In a mixing bowl, sift together the flour, ground hazelnuts, and cocoa. Zest the clementines over the mixture. Cut the clementines in half, press them, and pour the juice (about 7 tablespoons/100 ml) into the mixing bowl. Add the eggs and mix to obtain a ball of dough. Cover with a cloth and leave to rest for 30 minutes.

▣ Prepare your machine to roll out and cut the pasta. Divide the ball of dough into two parts. Sprinkle both halves with cocoa and pass them gradually through the rollers to obtain 1⁄16-in (2-mm) -thick layers of pasta. Then, put them through the other rollers to cut the dough into fettuccine (3⁄16 in or 5 mm wide).

▣ If you do not have a pasta machine, sprinkle your work surface and rolling pin with cocoa. Use the rolling pin to roll out the dough to a thickness of approximately 1⁄16 in (2 mm), then cut into strips 10 to 12 in (25 to 30 cm) long by 3⁄16 in (5 mm) wide with a large knife.

▣ Dry the fettuccine strands by hanging them over the wooden spoon handles for approximately 1 hour. Pile the pasta onto a tray and cover with a cloth.

For the chocolate cream

▣ Chop both types of chocolate and set aside in a mixing bowl. In a saucepan, bring the milk and heavy cream to a boil. Whisk the egg yolks in a mixing bowl. Pour one-third of the boiling liquid over the yolks, whisking vigorously, then return this mixture into the remainder in the saucepan. Cook as a custard to reach a temperature of 181°F/83°C, stirring constantly with a rubber spatula. Strain immediately, pouring the mixture directly over the chocolate. Leave to melt for 2 minutes. Whisk gently, working from the center outwards to obtain a smooth, velvety cream.

▣ Divide the warm cream into small bell-shaped bowls (about 3 tablespoons/40 g per person). You will serve the rest separately. Refrigerate for 3 hours.

For the reduced clementine juice

▣ Zest 4 of the clementines. Cut all 9 fruits in half and extract their juice (about 1¼ cups/300 ml). Set aside. In a saucepan, cook the sugar dry to obtain a golden caramel. Add the juice and zest. Bring to a boil and cook for several minutes until syrupy. Leave to cool, then pour in the Grand Marnier® and stir. Remove from the heat.

Presentation

▣ Store the bar of white chocolate in a place at 72°F/22 to 23°C. Once the smooth part has softened very slightly, scrape the pastry cutter along the entire length of the chocolate bar at a slight angle to form perfect shavings. Place them delicately in a small bowl. You can also grate the chocolate to imitate Parmesan cheese. Refrigerate until time to serve.

▣ Remove the chocolate creams from the refrigerator 15 minutes before serving. Warm up the reserved clementine juice.

▣ In a large saucepan, boil 3 quarts (3 liters) of water with the bay leaves. Cook the pasta 2 to 3 minutes (no longer). Drain the pasta and arrange on top of the chocolate creams. Serve immediately with the shaved or grated white chocolate and the warm clementine juice.

Buon appetito!

Island Chocolate Bars

Makes 6 chocolate bars, 3½ oz (100 g) each

Preparation time: **2 hours**

Resting time: **1 hour 30 minutes**

Cooking time: **20 minutes**

FROM THE STORES

2 cups (180 g) desiccated coconut (1⅓ cups +
⅔ cup or 120 g + 60 g)

½ cup + 2 tablespoons (120 g) superfine
granulated sugar

3 tablespoons (50 ml) water

2 limes

18 oz (500 g) milk chocolate 35% to 40%
minimum cocoa

KITCHEN UTENSILS

Electronic thermometer

Stainless steel spatula

Microplane grater

Chocolate bar molds (available at specialty
cake-making stores) or plastic box,
approximately 20 × 8 cm (8 × 3 in), covered
with parchment paper

Rolling pin

1 sheet acetate

Parchment paper

DIRECTIONS

For the coconut-lime nougatine

◙ Preheat the oven to 355°F/180°C. Toast the desiccated coconut to a light brown color. Leave to cool. Measure out 4¼ oz (120 g) toasted coconut; set aside the remainder.

◙ In a saucepan, cook the sugar and water to 320°F/160°C to obtain a nicely colored caramel. Add the 1⅓ cups (120 g) of toasted coconut while stirring vigorously with the stainless steel spatula.

◙ Pour the hot nougatine onto a sheet of parchment paper, cover with a second sheet, then roll it out as thinly as possible using the rolling pin. Leave to cool. Crush the nougatine with the rolling pin to obtain pieces the size of large bread crumbs. Set aside.

For the chocolate bars

◙ Zest the limes finely with the grater.

◙ Break up the chocolate and melt in a bain-marie until the temperature reaches 104°F/40°C. Remove from the heat.

◙ Temper the chocolate (see page 142) to give it the shine and the crispness of a good chocolate.

Once it has reached a usable temperature (84°F/29°C), add the remaining toasted coconut and the lime zest to the chocolate. Stir carefully. Pour the mixture into the chocolate bar molds (about 3½ oz/ 90 to 100 g per mold), or pour all of it into a plastic box. Tap the molds, or box, gently to remove air bubbles and, before the chocolate sets, sprinkle the surface of each bar with the coconut nougatine. Leave to crystallize for approximately 1 hour at 64°F/18°C. Then refrigerate for 30 minutes at 36°F/2°C.

◙ Carefully remove from the molds.

These island chocolate bars should be stored at a temperature of 61 to 64°F/16 to 18°C.

A **word** from **Gilles** Marchal

Enjoy these chocolate bars crushed over coconut ice cream or tropical fruit sorbet.

You can also try replacing the lime with another citrus fruit, and the coconut with small pieces of nut or dried fruit (hazelnuts, almonds, figs, raisins, walnuts, etc.). The coconut (from *coco*, which means "ghost" in Portuguese because of its shape, its three small holes, and hairy "head") got its name from the children of Portuguese colonists who settled on the islands in the Indian Ocean.

Above: Cocoa pods
Opposite: Golden beans in the sun

Fresh Berries with **Salvador** Ganache-Slide

Serves 6

Preparation time: **2 hours**

Resting time: **3 hours**

Cooking time: **30 minutes**

FROM THE **STORES**

For the ganache

6½ oz (180 g) dark chocolate 60% cocoa

¼ cup, or about 1 oz (30 g) fresh raspberries

7 tablespoons (100 ml) heavy cream

2 tablespoons (30 g) unsalted butter

For the raspberry juice

4 cups, or about 18 oz (500 g) fresh
    raspberries

½ Bourbon vanilla bean

7 tablespoons (100 ml) mineral water

3 tablespoons packed (40 g) brown sugar

½ oz (10 g) gelling agent for jam

10 twists of the Szechuan pepper grinder

Presentation

9 oz (250 g) Gariguette strawberries

1 cup, or about 4½ oz (125 g) fresh raspberries

2 cups (500 ml) Bourbon vanilla ice cream

KITCHEN UTENSILS

6 attractive glasses

Small dish or plastic box, ½ in
    (1½ cm) tall

Hand-held immersion blender

Cheesecloth or fine-mesh, conical strainer

Whisk

Clean cloth

Plastic wrap

DIRECTIONS

For the ganache

◉ Finely chop the chocolate and set aside in a mixing bowl. Mash the raspberries. In a saucepan, bring the heavy cream to a boil. Strain the raspberry juice into the cream, stir, and pour over the chocolate. Leave the chocolate to melt for 2 minutes, then whisk lightly in small circles, starting from the center. When the ganache thickens, move the whisk toward the sides of the bowl until you obtain a smooth texture. Gradually add the butter, in little pieces, and continue to mix gently, to obtain a silky, glossy ganache. Pour the ganache into the dish or box lined with plastic wrap. Refrigerate for 3 hours.

For the raspberry juice

◉ Put the raspberries and the vanilla bean (split in half lengthwise, seeds scraped) into a bain-marie; add 3 tablespoons (50 ml) of water. Cover and cook over medium heat, without stirring, for approximately 40 minutes.

Line the strainer with a clean cloth and place it over a container. Pour in the raspberries, fold the cloth over them, and place a weight on top to press the fruit and extract as much juice as possible; you should obtain approximately 1 cup (250 ml). Add the mineral water to make 1 cup + 2 tablespoons (300 ml). Mix the sugar and gelling agent, and add to the raspberry juice. Heat the mixture in a saucepan, then boil for approximately 10 minutes to thicken. Add the freshly ground pepper.

Presentation

◉ Chill 6 attractive glasses in the freezer to frost them. Rinse the strawberries in fresh water. Set aside 6 of the best-looking strawberries with stems for decoration. Remove the stems from the remaining berries and cut them in half. Cut the ganache into rectangles approximately 1 × ⅜ in (3 × 1 cm). Warm the raspberry juice.

◉ Place 1 small scoop of ice cream in the bottom of each glass. Add alternating layers of strawberries and raspberries. Top off the fruit with 1 or 2 rectangles of ganache. In front of your guests, pour the warm pepper and raspberry juice over the ganache so that it melts slightly. Enjoy immediately.

A **word** from **Gilles** Marchal

Salvador ganache is one of the best-selling creations invented by Robert Linxe thirty years ago. I've reinterpreted this chocolate indulgence with a new presentation to showcase the first berries of spring, adding the creamy sweetness of vanilla ice cream and, most importantly, creating a touch of drama by pouring peppered raspberry juice over the ganache to slightly melt both the chocolate and ice cream. If you don't have time to prepare this ganache yourself, however, fear not: simply find it at La Maison du Chocolat.

Crazy Chocolate Characters in Traditional Praline

Makes 12 large characters
Preparation time: **3 hours**
Resting time: **1 hour**
Cooking time: **15 minutes**

FROM THE STORES

1 cup (200 g) superfine granulated sugar
¼ cup (60 ml) mineral water
7 oz (200 g) lightly salted, shelled peanuts
3½ oz (100 g) whole blanched almonds
8 oz (250 g) dark chocolate 55% cocoa or
　　milk chocolate 35% to 40% cocoa

Presentation
Mixture of sugary cereals

KITCHEN UTENSILS

Food processor
Electronic thermometer
Plastic molds (a variety of animal shapes such
　　as dogs)
Stainless steel decorating spatula or
　　long knife
Piping bag with No. 8 (⁵⁄₁₆ in) round tip
Cotton balls
Parchment paper

DIRECTIONS

For the peanut-almond praline

▣ In a saucepan, cook the sugar with the water to obtain a golden brown caramel. Add the peanuts and almonds. Stir thoroughly to coat the nuts completely with caramel. Spread out the nuts on a sheet of parchment paper and leave to cool.

▣ In a food processor, pulse about a third of the nuts to make as smooth a praline as you can.

▣ Add the rest and mix again, taking care to stop the food processor while the praline still has small pieces of nut the size of salt grains. Set aside at room temperature.

For the chocolate mold

▣ Temper the chocolate (see page 142 for the technique on tempering chocolate for use in molds or garnishes). You can use all sorts of molds for this recipe. The important thing is to keep an eye on the temperature of the chocolate when you use it; it should never go over 89°F/31 to 32°C for dark chocolate and 86°F/29 to 30°C for milk chocolate.

▣ Use a cotton ball to polish the inside of each mold to remove any impurities. Once the chocolate has reached the correct temperature, fill the molds to the brim. Turn them upside down over a container to remove the excess and leave space for practice. Using a long knife or stainless steel spatula, scrape off any chocolate that is outside of the mold. Leave to harden at room temperature 68°F/20°C. Fill the piping bag with praline and fill each mold, leaving a gap of ¹⁄₁₆ in (2 mm) empty from the edge of the mold.

▣ Pour in the melted chocolate to "trap" the praline. Smooth the surface carefully using a spatula, taking care to fill in any holes. Leave to solidify again for a few minutes before refrigerating the molds for 1 hour.

Presentation

▣ Remove the shapes from their molds and play around with them (as in the photo) for your children and their friends. Glue the animal shapes using chocolate. To keep them upright while the chocolate glue hardens, place a support behind each shape. Scatter a few pieces of sugary cereal around to resemble dog snacks!

A **word** from **Gilles** Marchal

These tasty characters can also be replaced by more modern shapes—balls, rectangles, or whatever you prefer. You can find chocolate molds in stores specializing in cake- and chocolate-making utensils (I've listed my favorite stores at the end of the book). You can also try the plastic molds that come with children's modeling clay. Be sure not to use molds that are too deep, because the chocolates will be filled with too much praline and difficult to remove. Try using different flavors: dark or milk chocolate with almond-hazelnut, almond-pine nut or almond-walnut praline.

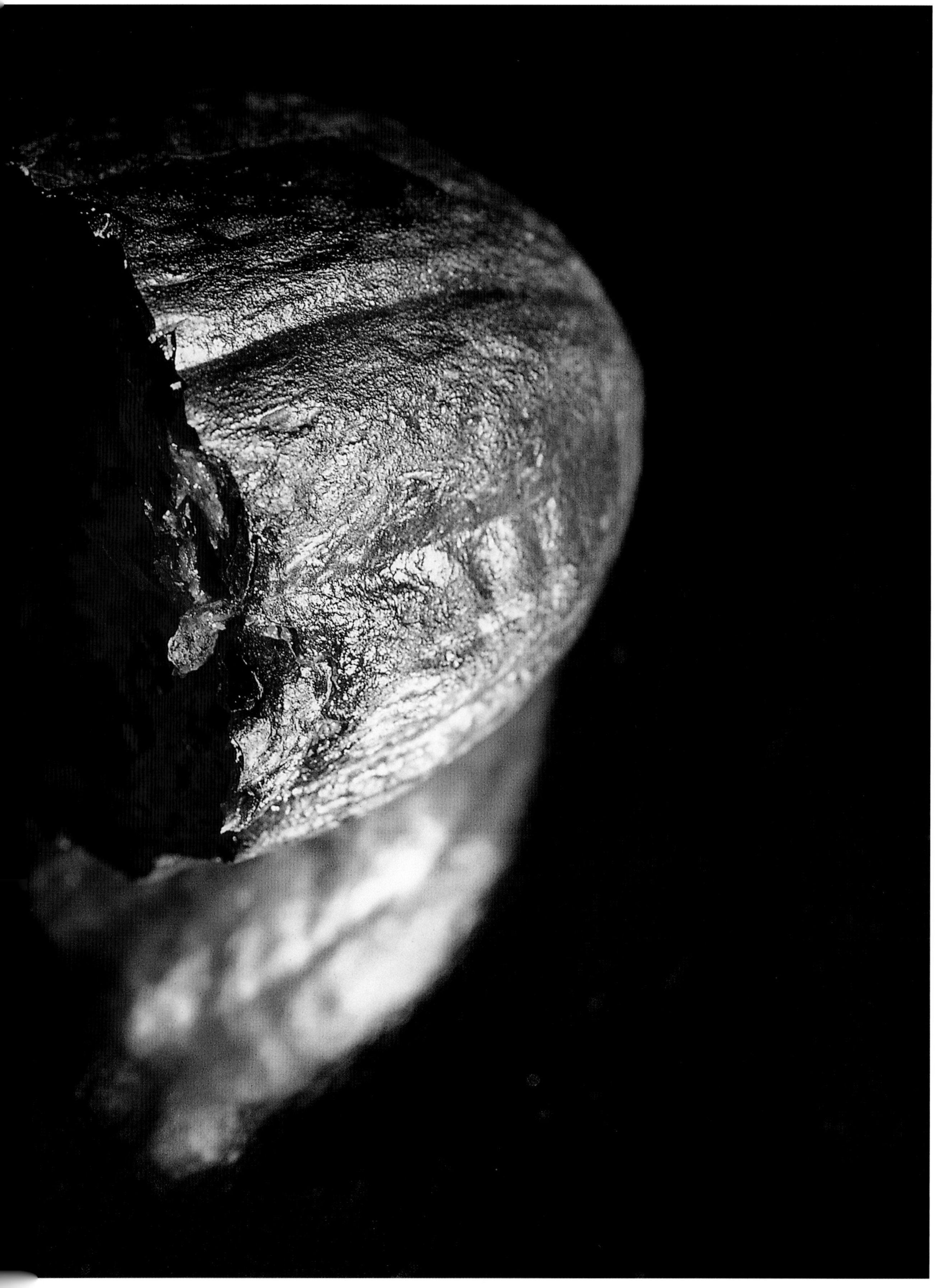

A Wave of Ganache Cream

Serves 6

Preparation time: **20 minutes**

Resting time: **2 hours**

Cooking time: **15 minutes**

FROM THE STORES

For the caramel

2 tablespoons (30 ml) heavy cream

⅓ cup (60 g) superfine granulated sugar

For the ganache cream

6 oz (170 g) dark chocolate 60% cocoa

¾ oz (20 g) milk chocolate 35% to 40% cocoa

7 tablespoons (100 ml) heavy cream

½ cup + 2 tablespoons (150 ml) whole milk

Seasoning and presentation

Szechuan peppercorn in grinder

1 brioche (from your local bakery)

KITCHEN UTENSILS

2 attractive glasses or jam jars

Whisk

DIRECTIONS

For the caramel

▣ In a saucepan, bring the heavy cream to a boil. Cook the sugar dry in a separate saucepan, stirring occasionally, to obtain a nice dark caramel. Remove from heat, then pour the hot cream over the caramel in several additions, stirring vigorously. Set aside.

For the ganache cream

▣ Finely chop both types of chocolate and set aside in a mixing bowl. In a saucepan, bring the heavy cream and milk to a boil. Pour over the caramel. Bring the mixture back to a boil, then pour over the chocolate. Leave the chocolate to melt for 2 minutes, then whisk lightly in small circles, starting from the center. When the ganache thickens, move the whisk toward the sides of the bowl until you obtain a smooth texture.

▣ Divide the warm ganache between your glasses or jars. Do not cover. Leave to cool for 1 hour, then set aside in the refrigerator. Remove 15 minutes before serving. Slice your brioche, spread the ganache cream over it, and enjoy!

A word from Gilles Marchal

For breakfast, try spreading this delicious cream on slices of panettone.

At lunch, treat yourself to pastry puffs filled with ganache.

As an afternoon snack, enjoy it on a slice of lemon cake.

At dinnertime, melt the ganache and pour over ice cream served with warm poached fruits.

In the evening, indulge in pure ganache with grated ginger or ground pepper spread over a cinnamon shortbread cookie. Sheer luxury!

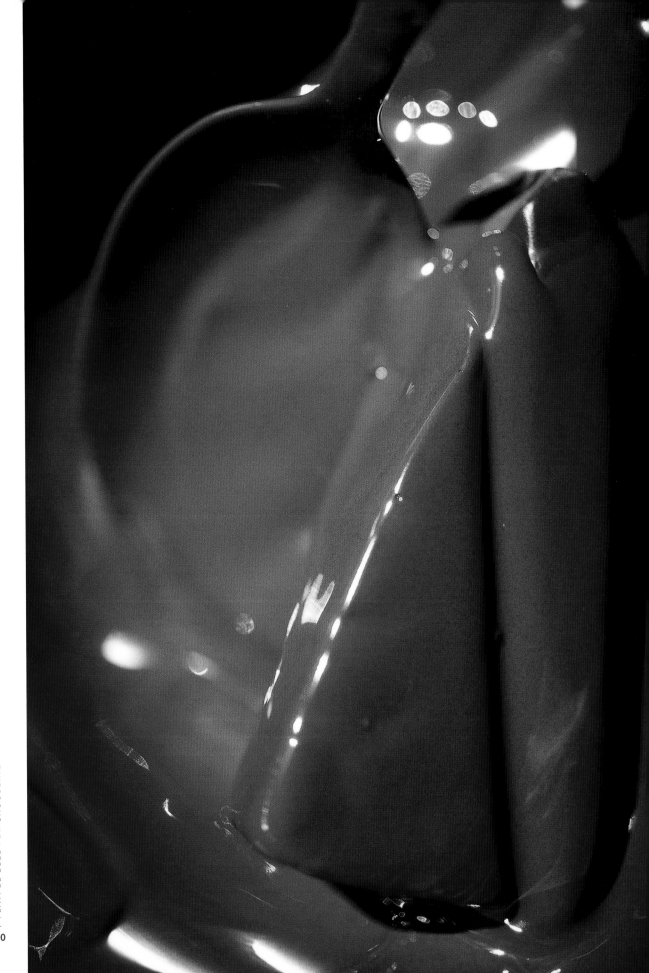

Above: Drawn chocolate
Opposite: Flooded spoon

Tropical Chocolate Velouté

Serves 6
Preparation time: **1 hour**
Cooking time: **15 minutes**

FROM THE STORES

9 oz (250 g) dark chocolate 60% cocoa
2½ cups (600 ml) whole milk
3 tablespoons packed (40 g) brown sugar
1 Tahitian vanilla bean
¾ cup (200 ml) coconut milk
7 tablespoons (100 ml) fresh pineapple juice
7 tablespoons (100 ml) fresh mango juice
3 tablespoons (50 ml) fresh passion fruit juice
2 small pinches freshly grated nutmeg
2 limes

KITCHEN UTENSILS

Microplane grater
Whisk
Juice extractor (or blender)

DIRECTIONS

◧ Finely chop the chocolate and set aside in a mixing bowl. In a saucepan, bring the milk to a boil with the brown sugar and the vanilla bean, split lengthwise, seeds scraped. Add the coconut milk, fruit juices, and nutmeg. Bring back to a boil, then remove from the heat.

◧ Zest the limes over this mixture. Remove the vanilla bean. Pour over the chopped chocolate. Leave to melt for 2 minutes. Beat vigorously to obtain a sauce with an even consistency. Transfer the milk, chocolate, and fruit juice mixture to the saucepan and simmer for approximately 10 minutes, stirring from time to time, to obtain a velvety consistency.

Serve warm in bowls or soup dishes.

A **word** from **Gilles** Marchal

For a more natural, authentic taste, purchase fresh fruit. Once you have peeled it, use the juicer (or blender) to obtain extra-fresh juice. This surprising velouté with its exotic flavors will go perfectly with your favorite ice cream or sorbet. Try adding some crunch by sprinkling it with coconut nougatine, caramelized pecans, or crunchy meringue. The velouté will keep quite well in the refrigerator for 2 days. Reheat it in a bain-marie to prevent it from thickening too much.

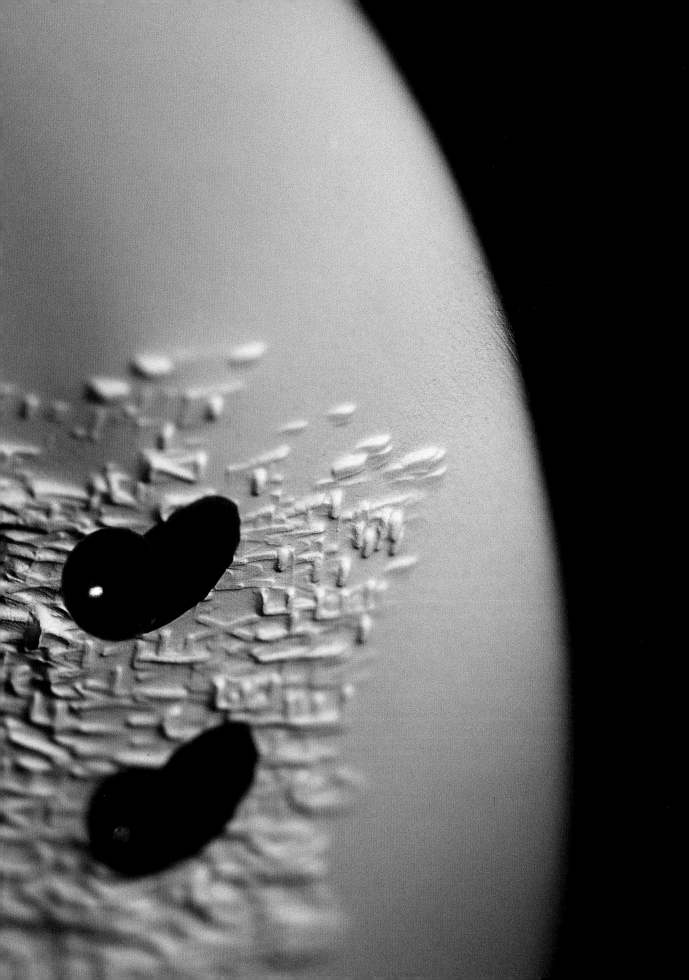

Sprinkled
with salt

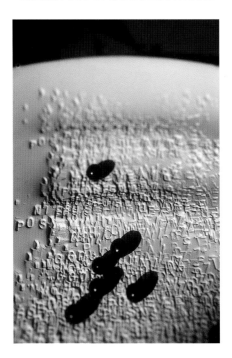

Élodie Rousselot

Thinking about objects and how they can be set is the foundation of Élodie Rousselot's creative approach. The earthenware factories in Gien offered the perfect location for her to experiment with the technical possibilities of this project. Élodie's work focuses on the concepts of composition and recomposition. "In this delicately balanced chaos, these earthenware dishes tell a story and absorb the experience of the lives around them, so a plate will always retain echoes of conversations."

For La Maison du Chocolat, she created nonenameled earthenware dishes. The chocolate caresses the objects, wrapping the plate in a veil of seduction.

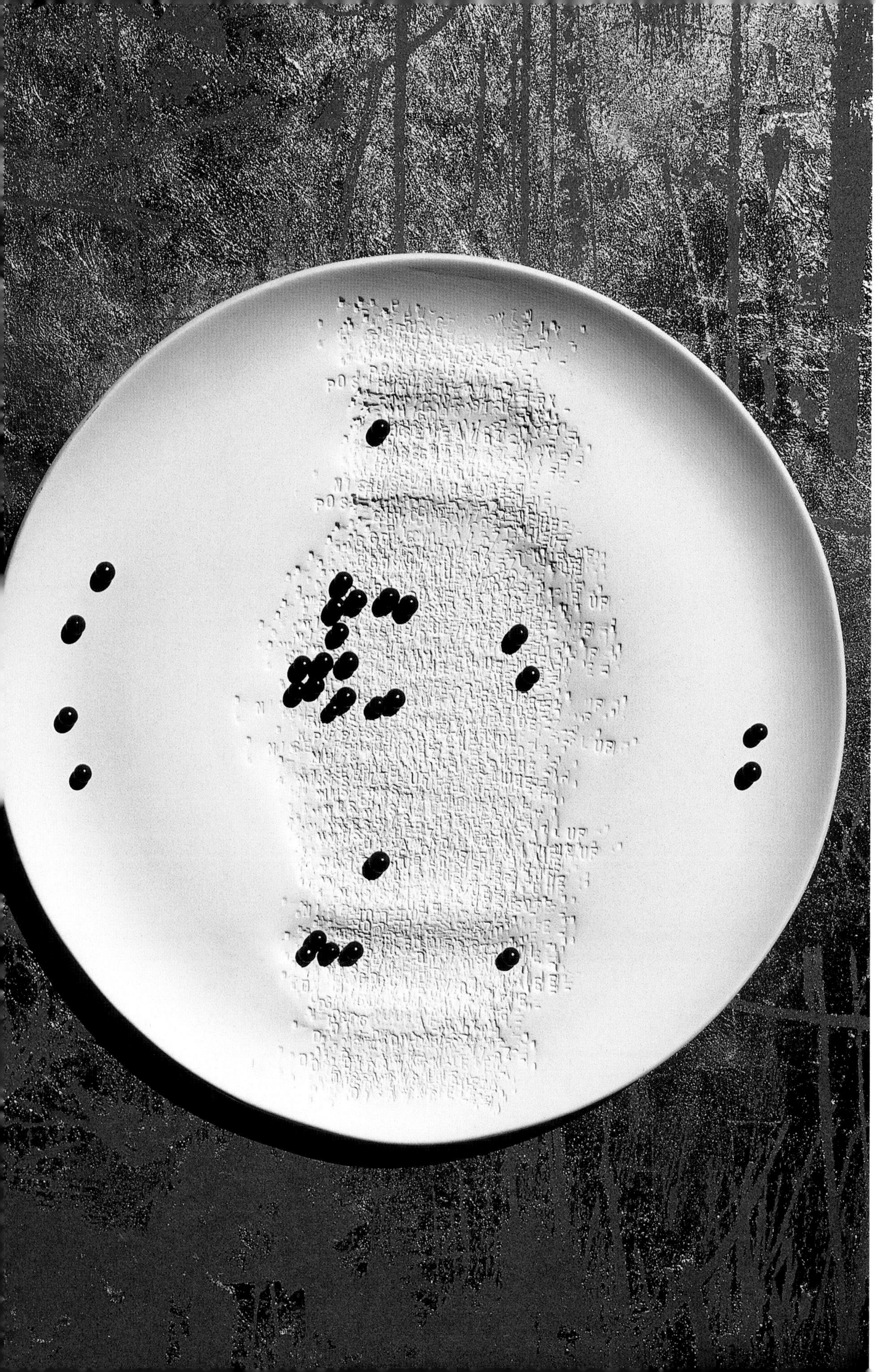

Warm **Chistera Ganache** with Roasted **Banana Peppers**

Serves 6
Preparation time: **1 hour**
Cooking time: **20 minutes**

FROM THE **STORES**

For the ganache

9 oz (250 g) sweet, red banana peppers

2 tablespoons (25 ml) balsamic vinegar
  of Modena

1 pinch Espelette pepper

3½ oz (100 g) milk chocolate 35% to
  40% cocoa

1¾ oz (200 g) dark chocolate 60% cocoa

7 tablespoons (100 ml) heavy cream

3 tablespoons + 2 teaspoons (40 g)
  unsalted butter

1 tablespoon acacia honey

5 twists of the black pepper mill

Presentation

24 red peanuts (peanuts with skin on)

12 cashew nuts

KITCHEN UTENSILS

6 small, attractive glasses

Hand-held immersion blender

Whisk

DIRECTIONS

For the ganache

▣ Wash and dry the peppers. Put them under the grill and roast each side completely. While the peppers are still hot, remove their stems, then peel them. Split the peppers in half, and discard the seeds and white ribs. Blend the flesh to a pulp (about 5½ oz/150 g), then add the vinegar and Espelette pepper. In a saucepan, bring the mixture to a boil and cook for 4 minutes. Set aside.

▣ Finely chop all of the chocolate and set aside in a mixing bowl. In a saucepan, bring the heavy cream to a boil with the honey and the ground black pepper. Add the banana pepper pulp and remove from the heat. Pour the warm pepper cream over the chocolate. Leave to melt for 2 minutes without touching. Using a whisk, gently stir in small circular movements, starting from the center. When the ganache thickens, work the whisk outwards toward the sides. Add the butter and mix carefully; you should obtain a ganache that due to the pepper pulp, is slightly fibrous.

Presentation

▣ Place 2 or 3 peanuts and 1 or 2 cashew nuts in the bottom of several attractive glasses. Pour 2 tablespoons of Chistera ganache soup over the nuts. Serve warm and enjoy with teaspoon in hand.

A **word** from **Gilles** Marchal

Here's a game to warm up your friends' taste buds: ask them to guess what flavors are in the ganache. Their answers will be just as surprising as the original, subtle taste of this chocolatey treat, best served to accompany an aperitif, such as Côtes du Roussillon 1903 Roc des Anges. If you'd rather serve the ganache as dessert, you can replace the pepper pulp with black currant pulp, and the peanuts with pistachios, pine nuts, or other nuts.

I recommend making this ganache at the last minute, since the surprise is enhanced when the soup is still warm and liquidy.

Foie Gras Cubes with Dried Fruit Chutney

Makes approximately 30 foie gras cubes

Preparation time: **1 hour 30 minutes**

Resting time: **24 hours**

Cooking time: **45 minutes**

FROM THE **STORES**

**For the foie gras (to be prepared at least
5 days before eating)**

1 whole duck foie gras (about 21 oz/600 g)

1¼ teaspoons (8 g) table salt

1 teaspoon (2 g) freshly ground pepper

2 teaspoons (10 ml) aged red port

For the chutney

½ cup (50 g) chopped almonds

⅓ cup (50 g) dried currants

¼ cup (30 g) dried cranberries

2 oz (60 g) soft dried apricots

6 Medjool dates

6 dried figs (Raphia variety)

2 teaspoons (10 ml) balsamic vinegar

Presentation

¼ oz (10 g) unsweetened cocoa powder

1¾ oz (50 g) dark chocolate 65% cocoa

KITCHEN UTENSILS

Porcelain terrine with lid, 6 in (15 cm) long

Electronic thermometer

Thick cardboard (cut to fit the inside of
    your terrine)

A weight of about 2¼ lb (1 kg) (a 1-quart or
    1-liter carton of milk, for example)

Plastic wrap

Small spoon

A **word** from **Gilles** Marchal

Making this delicious dish yourself is a true pleasure! Choose raw foie gras that is very firm and light in color. For easier preparation and to save time, you can purchase cooked foie gras; then all you have to do is cut the meat into cubes. Dried cranberries, a familiar sight in American grocery stores, are now beginning to make their way to markets in Europe. Medjool dates originate from Morocco; they are less sweet than other dates, pulpy and packed with flavor.

DIRECTIONS

For the foie gras

▣ The day before cooking: remove the foie gras from the refrigerator 1 hour before beginning to prepare the recipe, and leave it at room temperature.

▣ Use a sharp knife blade to slice open the two lobes from top to bottom, starting with the rounded end. "Denerve" them gently by pulling on the large vein and pinching it between your finger and the knife tip, which will help to remove the smaller veins as well; no blood should remain. Once the lobes are open, salt and pepper the insides evenly. Drizzle with aged port. Put the two halves of each lobe back together, with the seasoned portion on the inside. Place them in your terrine, tamping down very gently; they should fill the terrine to within ¾ in (2 cm) of the top. Cover the terrine and refrigerate for 24 hours.

▣ The day you make the recipe: Preheat the oven to 250°C/120°C. Place the terrine in a bain-marie (about one-third should be immersed in water) and put in the oven. Bake for 40 to 45 minutes, checking the temperature with an electric thermometer; it must not exceed 125°F/52°C.

▣ Remove the terrine from the oven and from the bain-marie. Leave to rest for 30 minutes.

▣ Place the terrine on a dish. Remove the lid. Wrap the cardboard with several layers of plastic wrap and place it over the foie gras. Set the 2¼-lb (1-kg) weight on top to press the foie gras down and force out the fat. Set aside in the refrigerator for another 6 hours.

▣ Carefully remove the cardboard from the foie gras and collect the excess fat. Heat it slightly in a saucepan.

▣ Clean the edges and outside of the terrine. Cover the entire surface of the terrine with a ⅛-in (3-mm) layer of liquid fat. Cover with the lid and return the terrine to the refrigerator for 3 to 4 days.

▣ The day of the meal: cut the foie gras into slices ⅜ in (1 cm) thick, then cut into 30 ⅜-in (1-cm) cubes. Set aside in the refrigerator.

For the chutney

▣ The day before the meal: dry roast the chopped almonds for a few minutes in a frying pan or an oven set to 300°F/150°C.

▣ Wash the other dried fruits, shake off any excess water, and pat dry. Cut into very small cubes (1/16 in or 2 mm per side). Combine with the almonds and balsamic vinegar. Refrigerate the mixture for 24 hours in an airtight container.

Presentation

▣ Remove the cubes of foie gras and the chutney from the refrigerator. Leave for 10 minutes to return to room temperature, then roll each cube in the chutney, pressing gently on the sides to make sure it sticks to the foie gras. Arrange on a plate. Sprinkle lightly with cocoa.

▣ Break up the chocolate into small pieces and melt it. Using a small spoon, drizzle melted chocolate over the cubes of foie gras. Store in the refrigerator until it is time to serve them.

Freshly **Thymed Scallops** with **Cocoa Nibs**

Serves 6

Preparation time: **2 hours**

Resting time: **3 hours (for the vinaigrette)**

Cooking time: **2 minutes**

FROM THE **STORES**

For the vinaigrette

Several leaves fresh tarragon

Several leaves flat-leaf parsley

8 tablespoons Corsican olive oil (Domaine de
  Marquiliani)

1 teaspoon hazelnut oil

1 teaspoon walnut oil

1 tablespoon balsamic vinegar

1 tablespoon sherry vinegar

1 tablespoon raspberry vinegar

1 tablespoon whole-grain mustard

1 teaspoon hot mustard

2 pinches curry powder

1 tablespoon unsweetened cocoa powder

Table salt

5 peppercorn blend (a combination of
  black, white, green, pink, and Jamaican
  peppercorns)

For the Florentine

4 teaspoons (30 g) acacia honey

6 tablespoons (80 g) superfine
  granulated sugar

7 tablespoons (100 ml) heavy cream

7 teaspoons (20 g) unsalted butter

1½ oz (40 g) diced candied orange peel

1½ oz (30 g) flaked almonds

1 oz (20 g) chopped almonds

2 sprigs fresh thyme

For the scallops

18 fresh scallops in their shells

Unsalted butter

Cocoa nibs (roasted cocoa beans crushed into
  small pieces, available at specialty food
  and cake-making stores)

Guérande sea salt

Coarsely ground black pepper

Presentation

Mixed baby salad leaves

Adzuki bean sprouts (available in health-food
  stores)

Arugula sprouts (available in health-food
  stores)

2 branches fresh coriander

1 sprig fresh thyme

KITCHEN UTENSILS

Nonstick pan

Electronic thermometer

Parchment paper or nonstick silicone mat

Shaker jar

Fork

Knife with flat blade

DIRECTIONS

For the vinaigrette (to be prepared the day before)

▣ Wash, dry, and finely chop the fresh herbs. Pour all the other ingredients for the vinaigrette into a mixing bowl, stir vigorously, and add the herbs. Store the vinaigrette in a shaker jar.

For the Florentine

▣ In a saucepan, cook the honey with the sugar, heavy cream, and butter to a temperature of 240°F/115°C. Off the heat, add the diced candied orange peel, the almonds, and the thyme leaves. Stir gently and leave to cool.
▣ Preheat the oven to 375°F/190°C.
▣ Spoon balls of Florentine the size of a cherry tomato onto a baking sheet covered with parchment paper or the nonstick silicone mat. Flatten slightly with a fork. Bake for 20 to 25 minutes until golden brown. Remove the Florentines from the oven and, using a non-serrated knife, shape each into a 1½-x-1½-in (4-x-4-cm) square. Set aside in a dry place.

For the scallops (to be seared at the last minute)

▣ Open each shell by running the blade of a long knife along the flat part. Remove the skirt and the viscera. Set aside the white scallop muscle (the coral can be pan-seared and served over basmati rice). Wash the scallops and dry using a clean cloth. Heat a nonstick pan over high heat and melt a large knob of butter. Add the scallops and sear for approximately 1 minute on each side; these shellfish can only be called a true delicacy if they remain tender in the center—scallops should be cooked quickly at high heat to prevent them becoming rubbery.

Presentation

▣ Arrange a few leaves of baby salad leaves with adzuki and arugula sprouts on each plate. Add the warm scallops and a few cocoa nibs. Sprinkle with chopped cilantro leaves and fresh thyme leaves. Drizzle the vinaigrette over the dish. Sprinkle with the freshly ground peppercorn blend, a few grains of sea salt, and cocoa nibs.

A **word** from **Gilles** Marchal

I love the contrast between the fresh salad, the crunchy sprouts, the delicate, seared scallops, and the wonderfully original vinaigrette. If you prepare it the day before, your vinaigrette will be even more pungent. I recommend experimenting with different herbs, spices, and even vinegars, oils, and mustards to create your own vinaigrette drawing on your personal favorite tastes.

Health-food stores and garden shops sell a wide variety of arugula, beetroot, adzuki, and other seeds—all you have to do is make them sprout! The cocoa and cocoa nibs are included for a very specific reason. They add crunch and just a hint of bitterness, and I treat them as spices. Cocoa nibs add an aromatic rather than a chocolatey note to your cooking. Try them with fish or grilled meat, too.

Black Olive **Phyllo Pockets**

Makes 30 small pastry pockets
Preparation time: **1 hour 30 minutes**
Resting time: **2 hours**
Cooking time: **10 minutes**

FROM THE **STORES**

For the chocolate, almond, hazelnut cream
1½ oz (40 g) dark chocolate 70% cocoa
6 tablespoons (80 g) unsalted butter
4 teaspoons (20 ml) Corsican olive oil
   (Domaine de Marquiliani)
¾ cup + 1 tablespoon (100 g) confectioners'
   sugar
6 teaspoons (10 g) unsweetened cocoa
   powder
¾ cup (70 g) ground almonds
¼ cup (30 g) ground hazelnuts
2 eggs (3½ oz/100 g)
2 tablespoons (30 ml) heavy cream

For the phyllo pockets
15 black olives (Cailletier)
6 soft dried apricots
6 sun-dried tomatoes
5 green cardamom pods
7 tablespoons (100 g) unsalted butter
30 square sheets brick or phyllo dough
   (4 × 4 in or 10 × 10 cm)
¼ cup (30 g) pine nuts
Confectioners' sugar

Presentation
Dark chocolate ganache (see recipe page 28)
30 attractive wooden skewers

KITCHEN UTENSILS
Whisk
Cherry pitter
Pastry brush
Piping bag with No. 8 (⁵⁄₁₆ in) round tip
Cheesecloth or fine-mesh, conical strainer
Plastic wrap

DIRECTIONS

For the chocolate, almond, hazelnut cream
◉ Chop the chocolate and melt in a bain-marie. In a mixing bowl, cream the butter with a wooden spoon until it is nearly liquid. Add the olive oil, confectioners' sugar, cocoa, ground almonds, ground hazelnuts, and eggs. Whisk gently to obtain an even consistency. Add the melted chocolate and stir carefully. Add the heavy cream. Cover the mixture with plastic wrap and refrigerate for 2 hours.

You can prepare this mixture the day before.

For the phyllo pockets
◉ Soak the olives in cold water for 2 hours to remove the excess salt. Dry and pit the olives, then cut them into large pieces. Cut the dried apricots and dried tomatoes into eight pieces each. Crush the cardamom pods and remove the seeds. Melt the butter. Spread out the sheets of phyllo dough on your work surface and brush them completely but lightly with melted butter.

◉ Preheat the oven to 390°F/200°C. Use the piping bag to form 1 ball of cream the size of a small walnut in the center of each sheet of phyllo. On top, arrange 1 piece each of apricot, tomato, and olive, 3 pine nuts, and 2 or 3 small cardamom seeds. Close the squares by folding two opposite sides one on top of the other, then fold in the remaining two sides underneath to form neat pockets. Place them on a baking sheet covered with parchment paper. Sprinkle with confectioners' sugar.
◉ Bake until evenly browned or for approximately 10 minutes.
◉ Serve the chocolate pockets warm on wooden skewers, accompanied by dark chocolate ganache.

You can make the pockets in the morning, store them in the refrigerator, and then bake them at the last minute.

A **word** from
Gilles Marchal

These morsels should be enjoyed like tapas. They combine different tastes and textures—crunchy and soft, sweet and acidic, sugary and bitter, floral and fruity, salty and spicy—all of my favorite tricks to surprise my guests' palates and put even the chattiest mouths to work chewing! With their intense flavor, these little *amuse-bouches* can also be served as dessert with a garnish of fresh thyme or basil ice cream, for example.

Corsican olive oil from the Domaine de Marquiliani is among the best in the world; it has a characteristic wild fruitiness and remarkable complexity. Similarly, Cailletier olives are one of the most sought-after varieties because of their crunch and strong aroma.

Above: Drizzle of cocoa nibs
Opposite: Phyllo pockets

Cocoa Nib **Sprinkle** on **Braised Veal** Sweetbreads

Serves 6

Preparation time: **3 hours**

Resting time: **2 hours**

Cooking time: **2 minutes for the veal sweetbreads, 3 hours for the veal stock**

FROM THE **STORES**

For the veal sweetbreads

6 veal sweetbreads, about 5½ oz (150 g) each

Ice cubes

Kosher salt

4 tablespoons (60 g) unsalted butter

3 tablespoons peanut oil

For the veal stock

18 oz (500 g) veal bones

3 tablespoons peanut oil

½ veal foot

2 large carrots

1 onion

½ leek

1 small shallot

1 clove pink garlic

1 plump tomato

1 sprig fresh thyme

2 fresh bay leaves

2 branches flat-leaf parsley

For the cocoa sauce

1 tablespoon cocoa nibs (roasted and crushed cocoa beans)

1 tablespoon Indian spice blend (whole)

1 pinch Guérande sea salt

2 teaspoons unsweetened cocoa powder

2 squares (10 g) dark chocolate 70% cocoa

Freshly ground black pepper

Presentation

Several dried garlic petals

Indian spice blend (whole)

Sea salt

Freshly ground pepper

KITCHEN UTENSILS

Weight, enameled casserole or Dutch oven, clean cloth, cheesecloth or fine-mesh strainer, heat-proof casserole

DIRECTIONS

For the veal sweetbreads

▣ The day before: as soon as you get back from shopping, place the veal sweetbreads in a large container. Immerse them completely in cool water, and soak for 24 hours in the refrigerator.

▣ The day of the meal: fill a large saucepan with water and bring to a boil with 1 teaspoon salt. Add the sweetbreads and blanch for 2 to 3 minutes. Remove them and plunge them immediately into a container full of water and ice cubes. Drain.

▣ Use a small knife to clean the sweetbreads, removing the nerves and small pockets of fat covering them. Roll them up in a clean cloth and refrigerate for 2 to 3 hours with a weight on top to press and slightly flatten them, which will make them easier to cook. Set aside in the refrigerator.

For the veal stock

▣ The day before: Preheat the oven to 400°F/200°C. Place the bones in an enameled casserole or Dutch oven, and drizzle with oil. Brown for several minutes. Cover with water and bring to a boil. Add the veal foot, the vegetables (peeled and cut into large pieces), and the herbs. Cover and simmer for 3 to 4 hours over low heat, adding water as necessary to ensure that the bones are always covered. Set aside in the refrigerator.

For the cocoa sauce

▣ The day of the meal: warm the veal stock and strain to obtain 2 cups (500 ml). Add the nibs, Indian spices, sea salt, cocoa, squares of chocolate, chopped, and a few twists of freshly ground black pepper. Mix together.

Cooking the veal sweetbreads

▣ Preheat the oven to 410°C/210°C.

▣ Heat the oil in a heat-proof casserole dish. Brown the sweetbreads evenly on each side. Add the butter and cocoa sauce. Bake the contents of the casserole for 8 minutes. Baste the sweetbreads frequently to coat them with juices and prevent them from drying out.

▣ Place the sweetbreads on the oven rack and collect the sauce; reduce it slightly in a saucepan. Adjust the seasoning if necessary.

▣ Serve your veal sweetbreads glazed with cocoa sauce. Garnish with 1 garlic petal, 1 pinch of Indian spices, several grains of sea salt, and 1 twist of freshly ground pepper.

A **word** from **Gilles** Marchal

Serve this dish with fresh pasta, crunchy green asparagus, and Parmesan shavings. Serve the remaining sauce separately. Try experimenting with cocoa nibs, unsweetened cocoa powder, or dark chocolate in your sauces, especially for meats. Used sparingly, chocolate adds a lovely bittersweet note. For me, crushed and roasted cocoa beans are first and foremost spices, and offer new avenues of flavors and aromas to be explored.

Stunning
Creations

Claire Colin

"I have had a weakness for sweets since I was small. My mouth watered as I worked with sugar, rose-flavored sweets, and chocolate in turn. I am also fascinated by lace paper and macramé and hope to design a line of sugary jewelry that could be worn or, even better, kept as mementos. To pay tribute to all of these delights, especially the licorice rolls I loved to uncoil, fold, and braid so much, I chose to use Scoubidou cords, which seemed the obvious choice because of their shine, flexibility, and deep black color, to design a collection of lacy treats in the form of bracelets, corsets, and tiaras.

Illustrating this recipe from Gilles Marchal has reunited me with one of my first loves: chocolate. I have made my personal dream of combining sweets with art a reality, and found huge enjoyment in creating a surprising piece out of an unusual material to astonish people and whet their appetites. This piece puts into practice the unlikely idea of creating a mouth-watering handbag that is as bitter and mysterious as chocolate lace."

Above: Claire Colin's Sac de nœud No. 1
Opposite: Gilles Marchal's Chocolatier's Handbag

Chocolatier's Handbags

Makes 6 handbags
Preparation time: **3 hours**
Resting time: **40 minutes**
No cooking required

21 oz (600 g) dark chocolate 55% cocoa
3½ oz (100 g) white "chocolate"
¾ oz (20 g) Matcha green tea powder
6 small gold or color-coated bead made
    of chocolate
1 edible gold leaf

KITCHEN UTENSILS
6 sheets acetate, 8 × 4 in (20 × 10 cm)
6 strips corrugated acetate, 4 × ⅜ in
    (10 × 1 cm)
Rubber pastry comb with prongs spaced
    about ⅛ in (3 mm) apart, available
    from DIY stores
Rectangular plate
Stainless steel decorating spatula or
    long, nonserrated knife
Parchment paper

A **word** from **Gilles** Marchal

This recipe demands more than a few tips from me—it's a test of true technical skill in the kitchen! I invented and designed this chocolate handbag for a top fashion designer who was giving a sneak preview of his catwalk show at the Le Bristol hotel bar. Be persistent: even I didn't pull it off the first time. The inside of the bag can be garnished with chocolate ice cream, iced parfait with orange zest, or warm, caramelized spiced fruits. For the first and only time in their lives, the models absolutely devoured a true "chocolate" handbag!

DIRECTIONS

▣ Prepare your acetate sheets: the larger ones will be used to make the dark chocolate bag, and the strips for the white chocolate "crocodile skin" decoration. Break both types of chocolate into pieces and melt them separately in saucepans in a bain-marie, taking care not to exceed 88 to 89°F/31 to 32°C for the dark chocolate and 80 to 82°F/27 to 28°C for the white chocolate. (See page 142 for the tempering method.)

▣ Grease your work surface very lightly to prevent the acetate sheets from slipping. Lay out 1 large acetate sheet in front of you lengthwise. Ladle a generous spoonful of chocolate onto the sheet, then smooth from bottom to top to cover the sheet completely with a layer 1/32 in (1 mm) thick. Before the chocolate sets, place the comb over it, leaving a band of 3/4 in (2 cm) on top. Pull the comb down toward the bottom. Use a small spoon to form a line of dark chocolate across the width of the sheet, halfway up the strips formed by the comb; this line of chocolate will reinforce what will eventually be the bottom of the bag. Scrape any excess chocolate off the work surface.

▣ Use the tip of a knife to lift the sheet from underneath and fold it lengthwise along the bottom of the bag, without making the fold too pronounced so that the bag keeps a rounded shape. Place the lower part over the strip left without comb marks at the top and "glue" using a small amount of melted chocolate applied with a knife, pressing gently; your handbag has its shape. Leave to solidify for 10 minutes before placing the bag on the plate. Set aside in the refrigerator.

▣ Make 5 more bags in the same way.

▣ On the sheet of parchment paper, while the dark chocolate is still liquid, use a spoon to form 12 circles each 2½ in (6 cm) in diameter that are not entirely closed; they will be the straps for your handbags. Place them in the refrigerator.

▣ Place a small amount of tea powder on the acetate strips (remove any excess with a finger) and then cover completely with a layer of tempered chocolate 1/16 in (2 mm) thick; this is the top of the bag, imitating shagreen or crocodile skin. Leave to harden in the refrigerator for 30 minutes.

▣ Carefully remove the acetate from the bags and gently pry the handles from the parchment paper. Remove the acetate strips as well, and use a small knife dipped in the tempered dark chocolate to "glue" them to the top of the bag as a clasp. Leave the bags to harden. Be careful—once the bags have been assembled, they are very fragile!

▣ Still using a touch of melted chocolate applied with a knife, "glue" one handle on to each side of the bag along with the chocolate beads. Rely on your own inspiration to arrange the gold leaf.

"Glue" the bags to the presentation plate using dark chocolate at 90°F/32°C. Refrigerate until time to serve. Serve with iced parfait made with orange zest, or warm, caramelized spiced fruits.

What's **Black and Pink** and **Dipped** in **Pink Champagne?**

Makes approximately 100 small cubes

Preparation time: **1 hour**

Resting time: **3 hours**

Cooking time: **10 minutes**

FROM THE **STORES**

For the four-berry tea ganache

4½ oz (125 g) milk chocolate 35% to 40% cocoa

1 oz (30 g) dark chocolate 70% cocoa

½ cup (120 ml) heavy cream

2 tablespoons loose berry-flavored tea (e.g. Dammann)

For cutting

½ cup (50 g) unsweetened cocoa powder

For the coating

5 oz (150 g) dark chocolate 70% cocoa

5 or 6 pinches green aniseed, ground to powder

Presentation

1 bottle rosé champagne (preferably, Laurent-Perrier)

KITCHEN UTENSILS

Electronic thermometer

Dish or plastic box measuring approximately 2½ × 5 in (6 x 12 cm)

Cheesecloth or fine-mesh strainer

Whisk

Plastic wrap or parchment paper

Wooden skewers

DIRECTIONS

◙ Chill the champagne.

For the four-berry tea ganache

◙ Chop both types of chocolate and set aside in a mixing bowl. In a saucepan, bring the heavy cream to a boil. Remove from the heat, add the tea, cover and steep for 8 minutes but no longer; this will infuse your ganache with the flavor of the tea without making it bitter. Strain, then heat to a boil. Pour the tea-infused cream over the chocolate, covering it completely. Leave the chocolate to melt for 2 minutes, then whisk lightly in small circles, starting from the center. When the ganache thickens, whisk the mixture outwards to the sides of the bowl to obtain a silky, glossy texture.

◙ Line the bottom and sides of your dish or box with plastic wrap. Pour in the liquid ganache to a depth of ½ in (1½ cm). Refrigerate for 3 hours, then freeze for 1 hour; this will make the ganache firm and easier to cut.

◙ Sprinkle your work surface lightly with cocoa. Flip the ganache over onto the surface and remove the plastic wrap. Cut into ½-in (1½-cm) strips, then into cubes. Skewer the cubes and present on small, attractive plates. Set aside in the refrigerator.

Presentation

◙ Break up the 5 oz (150 g) of dark chocolate and melt in a bain-marie until the temperature reaches 95°F/35°C. Add the powdered aniseed and keep the chocolate at the same temperature in the bain-marie.

◙ Just before serving, pour the chocolate into small bowls and place them in the center of the table. Serve the ganache cubes with a small flute of well-chilled champagne (40°F/4°C) for each guest. To enjoy, dip a cube of ganache in the melted chocolate, gently shake the excess, then dip into the glass of champagne; the cold champagne will solidify the chocolate. Leave for a few seconds to admire the bubbles that dance around the cube and raise it to the surface as if by magic, then savor this unique "truffle." Repeat as often as you like, and remember to enjoy your glass of champagne—responsibly of course!

A **word** from
Gilles Marchal

I came up with the idea to combine two extraordinary products—chocolate and rosé champagne—at La Maison du Chocolat's thirtieth-anniversary celebration held at the Salle Pleyel in October 2007. My luxurious take on fondue was born.

For children's birthdays, try replacing the champagne with a nonalcoholic fizzy beverage, and the ganache cubes with marshmallows, fresh fruit, or soft sweets—a treat they'll never forget!

Pear, Chocolate, and Black Truffle Winter Macarons

Makes 25 small macarons
Preparation time: **1 hour 15 minutes**
Resting time: **1 hour**
Cooking time: **20 minutes**

FROM THE STORES

For the macarons

1⅔ cups (200 g) confectioners' sugar

¾ cup + 1 tablespoon (80 g) ground almonds

7 tablespoons (40 g) ground walnuts

¾ cup (160 g) superfine granulated sugar

3 tablespoons (50 ml) mineral water

4 egg whites (about 4 oz/120 g)

1 pinch table salt

For the pear ganache

2 oz (60 g) canned pears packed in syrup, drained

1¾ oz (150 g) dark chocolate 65% cocoa

7 tablespoons (100 ml) heavy cream

2 tablespoons Etienne Brana Williams pear liqueur

Presentation

3 Perigord black truffles (*Tuber melanosporum*)

Williams pear liqueur

Guérande sea salt

KITCHEN UTENSILS

Fine-mesh strainer

Piping bag with No. 10 or No. 8 (⅜ or ⁵⁄₁₆ in) tip

Electronic thermometer

Electric mixer (whisk)

Hand-held immersion blender

Parchment paper

New toothbrush

A **word** from **Gilles** Marchal

These macarons can be enjoyed with an aged vintage port during the cheese course and served with Papillon® Roquefort, Stilton, or aged Cantal. This sophisticated treat is sure to arouse the most discerning palates.

One of my most cherished memories is of the fine morning I spent in Perigord hunting for black truffles. These culinary "diamonds" are delicately unearthed with the help of a pig or dog whose highly trained snout leads the hunters to these much-coveted mushrooms of incomparable flavor. The best harvests come from truffles growing four to five inches underground, usually in oak forests. You can find fresh truffles in specialty food stores from November to March.

DIRECTIONS

For the pear ganache

Mash the drained canned pears to obtain a pulp.

Finely chop the chocolate and set aside in a mixing bowl. In a saucepan, bring the heavy cream to a boil. Add the pear pulp and bring the mixture back to a boil. Pour over the chocolate. Leave the chocolate to melt for 2 minutes, then whisk lightly in small circles, starting from the center. When the ganache thickens, whisk the mixture outwards to the sides of the bowl to obtain a smooth texture. Add the liqueur and mix gently to obtain a silky, glossy ganache.

For the macarons

Using the toothbrush, carefully clean the truffles, without water, to remove any dirt. Cut into $\frac{1}{32}$-in (1-mm) thick slices. Set aside.

Preheat the oven to 300°F/150°C and cover a baking sheet with parchment paper. In a mixing bowl, sift the confectioners' sugar and the ground almonds and walnuts. In a saucepan, cook the superfine granulated sugar with the water to obtain a syrup. Once the temperature reaches approximately 220°F/105°C, begin beating two of the egg whites in the bowl of an electric mixer with a pinch of salt until they form very stiff peaks, while continuing to let the syrup cook. When the syrup reaches precisely 244°F/118°C, immediately drizzle it with care over the stiff egg whites, continuing to beat until you obtain a firm meringue. Add the sifted dry ingredients, then add the remaining egg whites while mixing. Continue to mix until the macaron dough is smooth; it should be glossy and form ribbons. Fill your piping bag with dough, using the No. 10 ($\frac{3}{8}$ in) tip for large macarons or the No. 8 ($\frac{5}{16}$ in) tip for small macarons.

Form balls of dough on the baking sheet, 2 in (5 cm) in diameter for large macarons or ¾ in (2 cm) for small ones. Bake large macarons for approximately 10 minutes, small for approximately 9 minutes; they should form a thin, crunchy shell on the top and sides, but remain soft in the center.

Leave to cool before flipping over. Spread pear ganache over half of the macaron shells. Lay a thin truffle slice on top, moisten slightly with pear liqueur, and sprinkle with 3 or 4 grains of sea salt. Glue the second half of the macaron on top of the truffle using a small amount of ganache. Chill the macarons for 2 hours. Remove 30 minutes before serving.

Jamaican Shortbread Topped with Caribbean Chocolate

Serves 6

Preparation time: **2 hours 30 minutes**

Resting time: **3 hours**

Cooking time: **30 minutes**

FROM THE **STORES**

For the shortbread

12 tablespoons (180 g) unsalted butter

½ cup + 2 tablespoons (70 g) confectioners' sugar

1 cup (100 g) ground almonds

2 pinches table salt

1 whole egg (1¾ oz/50 g)

1½ cups (200 g) finely ground flour

For the chocolate cream

6½ oz (180 g) dark chocolate minimum 70% cocoa

3 egg yolks (2 oz/60 g)

2 heaped tablespoons (30 g) superfine granulated sugar

½ cup (125 ml) whole milk

½ cup (125 ml) heavy cream

For the cocoa streusel

7 tablespoons (100 g) unsalted butter

½ cup packed (100 g) brown sugar

¾ cup (100 g) cake flour

½ cup (40 g) unsweetened cocoa powder

3 large pinches ground cinnamon

1½ cups (150 g) ground almonds

For the caramel emulsion

½ Tahitian vanilla bean

¼ cup (60 ml) hot water

½ cup (100 g) superfine granulated sugar

¾ cup (200 ml) heavy cream

Presentation

2 cups (½ liter) coffee bean ice cream

1¾ oz (50 g) blanched hazelnuts

Chocolate for drizzling

KITCHEN UTENSILS

Parchment paper; round pastry cutter 2 in (5 cm) diameter, or use a round glass; coarse cheese or box grater; rolling pin; cheesecloth or fine-mesh-conical strainer; plastic wrap or airtight container; pastry bag with No. 10 (⅜ in) round tip

A **word** from **Gilles** Marchal

Order your coffee bean ice cream from your local ice cream maker or La Maison du Chocolat. This "Jamaican" dessert (as Véronique Durruty dubbed it during the photo shoot) is also delicious topped with a quenelle of salted caramel or Bourbon vanilla ice cream.

I recommend making the dough two days ahead and baking it the day before, then storing the shortbread and streusel in a dry place. The chocolate cream can also be made the day before. That way, all that's left on the day is to piece the dessert together—giving you all the time in the world to prepare your meal and decorate your table.

DIRECTIONS

For the shortbread

◨ In a mixing bowl, cream the butter until it is very soft, almost liquid. Add the remaining ingredients. Knead to obtain a dough with an even consistency. Place the dough between 2 sheets of parchment paper. Roll out into a rectangle to a thickness of 3/16 in (5 mm). Leave to rest for 2 hours in the refrigerator.
◨ Preheat the oven to 300°F/150°C. Remove the top sheet of parchment paper from the dough and lay it over your work surface, then flip the dough over onto it. Remove the second sheet. Use the pastry cutter to form circles of dough and place them on a baking sheet covered with parchment paper. Bake for 20 to 25 minutes, until the shortbread cookies are browned on each side. Leave to cool, then store in a dry place.

For the chocolate cream

◨ Finely chop the chocolate and set aside in a mixing bowl. In another mixing bowl, beat the egg yolks with the sugar until the mixture turns a pale yellow color. In a saucepan, bring the milk and heavy cream to a boil, pour over the egg yolk–sugar mixture and then pour it all back into a saucepan.

Cook as though for a custard over low heat, stirring with a wooden spoon, to a temperature of 181°F/83°C: the cream should coat the back of the spoon. Strain the cream, then pour it over the chocolate. Leave to melt for a couple of minutes without stirring, then mix gently, working from the center toward the outside, to obtain a thick, glossy chocolate cream. Cover with plastic wrap or transfer into an airtight container and refrigerate a minimum of 3 hours. I recommend that you prepare the cream the day before to make sure that it is firm enough.

For the cocoa streusel

◨ In a mixing bowl, cream the butter until it is soft. Add the remaining ingredients. Knead to obtain a dough with an even consistency. Form the dough into a ball and refrigerate for 2 hours.
◨ Preheat the oven to 300°F/150°C. Cover the baking sheet with parchment paper. Remove the dough from the refrigerator. Use the cheese grater (the side with large holes) to grate the dough over the baking sheet to obtain large threads, taking care not to overlap them too much. Place in the oven without touching them (to avoid breakage) and bake for approximately 30 minutes. Leave to cool, then store in a dry place.

For the caramel emulsion

◨ Split the vanilla bean lengthwise, and, using the tip of a small knife, scrape out the seeds into the hot water. In a saucepan, cook the sugar dry, stirring occasionally, until it turns a warm caramel color. Deglaze the caramel by adding the vanilla-infused hot water and stirring vigorously to obtain a liquid caramel. Set aside at room temperature.
◨ In a mixing bowl, whisk the very cold heavy cream gently until it thickens somewhat. Add half of the cold caramel to flavor it. Set aside the rest for the presentation.

Presentation

◨ Use the piping bag to form a ball of chocolate on top of each shortbread cookie. Decorate with lovely threads of streusel. Crush the hazelnuts and arrange them in the center of the cream. Present the shortbread cookies on plates and, just before serving, top off the streusel with a scoop of coffee bean ice cream, then pour over the caramel emulsion. Add chocolate for decoration as desired.

Saffron and Chocolate Jackstraws

Makes 30 pastries

Preparation time: **1 hour 30 minutes**

Resting time: **3 hours**

Cooking time: **24 minutes**

FROM THE STORES

For the saffron cream

¾ cup (200 ml) whole milk

3 tablespoons (50 ml) heavy cream

½ Bourbon vanilla bean

5 pinches powdered Iranian saffron

3 tablespoons packed (40 g) brown sugar

¾ oz (20 g) flan or pasty cream powder

3 egg yolks (2 oz/60 g)

For the chocolate cream

5½ oz (160 g) dark chocolate 65% cocoa

½ cup + 2 tablespoons (150 ml) whole milk

7 tablespoons (100 ml) heavy cream

2 egg yolks (1½ oz/40 g)

4 teaspoons packed (20 g) brown sugar

For the caramelized pecans

½ cup (100 g) superfine granulated sugar

3 tablespoons (40 ml) mineral water

7 oz (200 g) shelled pecans

For the puff pastry

1 rectangle puff pastry dough made with
    butter (12 × 8 × ⅛ in thick or 30 × 20 cm ×
    3 mm thick)

Confectioners' sugar

Presentation

Iranian saffron threads

KITCHEN UTENSILS

Electronic thermometer

2 piping bags with No. 8 (⁵⁄₁₆ in) round tips

Fine-mesh strainer

Spatula

Parchment paper

Plastic wrap

A **word** from **Gilles** Marchal

Good puff pastry should melt in the mouth. I recommend that you buy the pastry dough (made with butter) from your local bakery or speciality store. Don't be afraid to bake the pastry until it turns an even caramel color.

The saffron adds a unique, incomparable flavor. Iranian saffron is the most delicately fragranced of them all. Harvested by hand before sunrise, no less than 120,000 flowers are needed to produce 1 kilogram (about 2¼ pounds) of saffron threads. While it's true that the rarest ingredients are also the most expensive, the pleasure you get from a rare treat is simply priceless.

DIRECTIONS

For the saffron cream

◉ In a saucepan, bring the milk and heavy cream to a boil with the vanilla bean (split in half lengthwise, seeds scraped) and 5 generous pinches of powdered saffron.

◉ In a mixing bowl, combine the sugar and flan powder; add the eggs and stir until the mixture turns a pale yellow color. Fold this mixture into the boiling milk. Stir vigorously, then cook as you would pastry cream for 1½ to 2 minutes after it comes to a boil. Pour the mixture into another container, remove the vanilla bean, and leave the cream to cool, stirring occasionally. Cover the container with plastic wrap and refrigerate until the mixture has cooled completely.

◉ You can prepare this cream the day before.

For the chocolate cream

◉ Chop the chocolate and set aside in a mixing bowl. In a saucepan, bring the milk and heavy cream to a boil. In a shallow bowl, gently beat the egg yolks and the sugar. Whisk vigorously and cook to 181°F/83°C, like a custard. Strain directly onto the chocolate pieces. Leave to melt for 2 minutes, then whisk together in a circular motion, working outwards from the center until you have a smooth, glossy cream. Leave to cool slightly. Cover the mixing bowl with plastic wrap and refrigerate for a minimum of 3 hours.

◉ You can prepare this cream the day before.

For the caramelized pecans

◉ In a saucepan, cook the sugar in the water. When the syrup begins to form large, thick, transparent bubbles, add the pecans, stirring with a spatula to cover them completely with sugar (so they crystallize). Continue to cook until the sugar becomes caramelized. Pour the caramelized nuts onto a piece of parchment paper and leave to cool, then smash into large pieces.

◉ The pecans can be prepared the day before and stored in an airtight container in a dry place.

For the puff pastry

◉ Preheat the oven to 400°F/200°C. Cut the dough into 6 x ¾-in (15 x 1½-cm) strips, and arrange them on a baking sheet covered with parchment paper, spaced 1½ in (3 cm) apart. Bake for approximately 20 minutes, until golden brown. Remove the baking sheet from the oven and increase the temperature to 480°F/250°C. Sprinkle the puff pastry strips generously with confectioners' sugar.

Return them to the oven for another 3 to 4 minutes, until the sugar melts, becoming transparent and crunchy. Leave to cool.

◉ You can bake the pastry sticks in the morning for an evening meal, and store them in an airtight container in a dry place.

Presentation

◉ Fill one piping bag with saffron cream and the other with chocolate cream.

◉ Form 3 small balls of saffron cream on the ends of 15 pastry sticks, and 3 small balls of chocolate cream on the other 15 pastry sticks. Arrange several saffron threads on the orange pastry sticks and several pieces of pecan on the chocolate ones. Serve the remaining cream separately.

Saffron and Chocolate Jackstraws

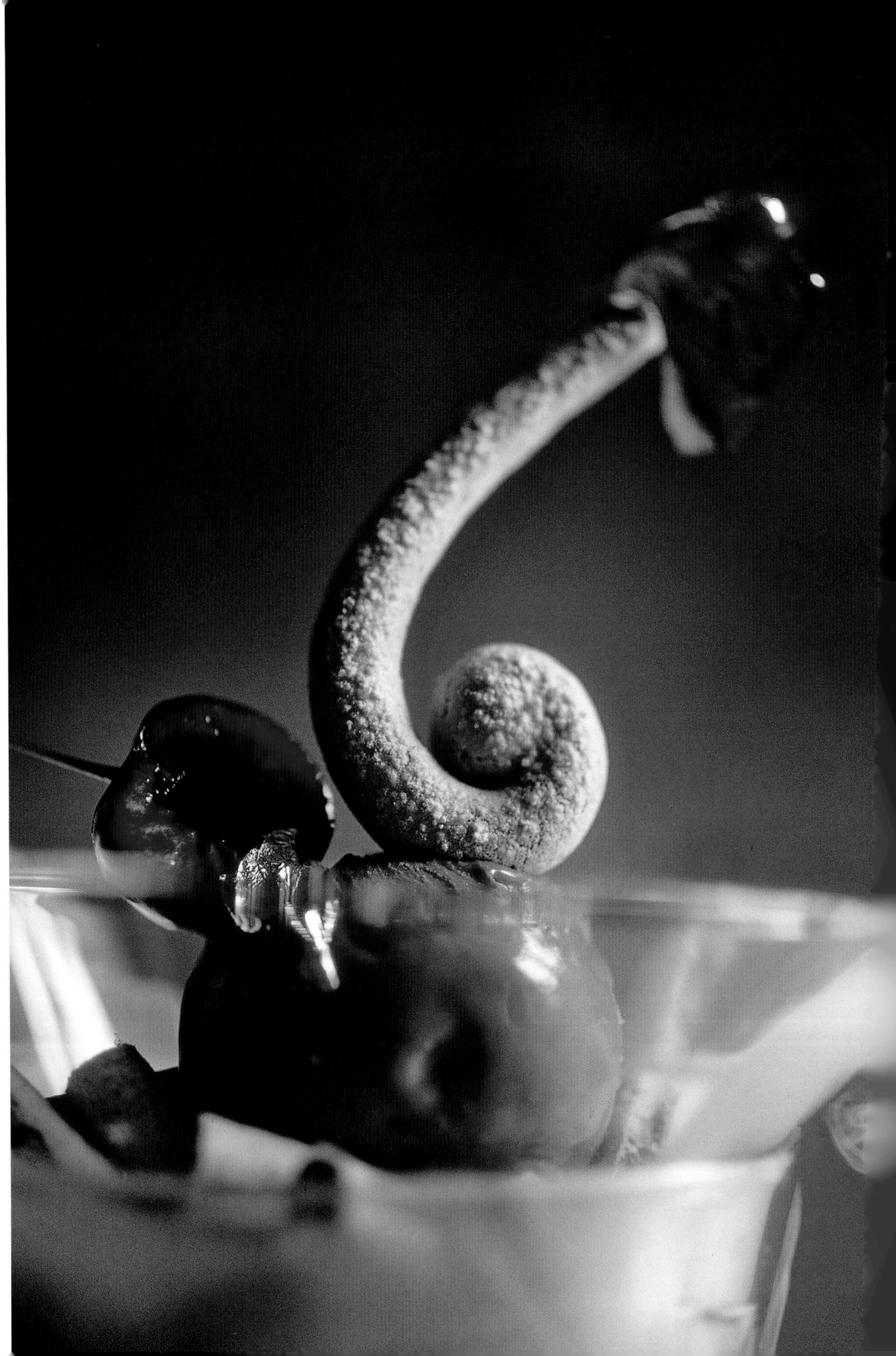

Bird's Beak **Meringues** in the **Mist**

Serves 6
Preparation time: **1 hour**
Cooking time: **1 hour 30 minutes**

FROM THE **STORES**

For the meringue

3 egg whites (3 oz/90 g)

1 pinch salt

6 tablespoons (80 g) superfine granulated
    sugar

½ cup + 2 tablespoons (70 g) confectioners'
    sugar

6 teaspoons (10 g) unsweetened cocoa
    powder

For the poached cherries

18 oz (500 g) Summit or Burlat cherries

2 tablespoons (30 g) unsalted butter

2 tablespoons packed (30 g) brown sugar

2 tablespoons aged Kirsch

Presentation

2 fl oz (50 ml) cherry syrup

2½ cups (600 ml) sparkling water

4 teaspoons (20 ml) barley water or orgeat
    syrup

2 cups (½ liter) chocolate ice cream (see
    recipe page 30)

Dry ice (optional)

KITCHEN UTENSILS

Piping bag with No. 6 (¼ in) round tip

Fine-mesh strainer

Cherry pitter

Electric mixer

Nonstick pan

6 tall, bell-shaped glasses

6 clear, conical glasses

Parchment paper

DIRECTIONS

For the meringue

▣ Preheat the oven to 300°F/150°C. Beat the egg whites until they form stiff peaks, adding a pinch of salt while mixing. When the egg whites are almost stiff, add the granulated sugar while you continue to beat the mixture to an even consistency. Add the sifted confectioners' sugar and cocoa, stirring carefully with a spoon. Cover a baking sheet with parchment paper, then use the piping bag to form parrot beak shapes approximately 4 in (10 cm) long, a bit like large commas (see photo). Lower the oven temperature to 210°F/100°C and bake the meringues for 1½ to 2 hours.

▣ Run a thin knife blade under the hot meringues to pry them gently from the paper. Once cool, store the meringues in an airtight container in a dry place.

For the poached cherries

▣ Wash the cherries. Set aside the 12 most luscious cherries with stems for the presentation. Remove the pits and stems from the remaining cherries.

▣ In a hot frying pan, melt the butter, then tip in the cherries. Add the sugar and cook over high heat for 2 to 3 minutes. Pour in the Kirsch, flambé, and leave on the heat.

Presentation

▣ Mix the cherry syrup, barley water or orgeat syrup, and sparkling water. Pour the mixture into the bottom of 6 tall, flared glasses. Drop 1 or 2 whole cherries into the liquid. Place a second, conical glass over each flared glass (see photo). Set aside the 6 most attractive meringue beaks, and cut the others into large pieces. Garnish the glasses with 2 large spoonfuls of poached cherries, a few pieces of crushed meringue, 1 scoop of chocolate ice cream, ½ fresh cherry, and 1 meringue bird's beak.

Serve immediately.

A **word** from **Gilles** Marchal

You can serve this dessert with whipped cream as a nod to the famous Black Forest: chocolate, whipped cream, and cherries flambéed in Kirsch.

For a spectacular effect, drop a piece of dry ice into the syrup to add a mysterious, magical dimension to your dinner party. Dry ice is extremely cold (-292°F/-180°C), so handle it carefully!

Bird's Beak Meringues in the Mist

Melting Chocolate Chickens

Makes 6 small chickens
Preparation time: **1 hour**
Resting time: **1 hour**
No cooking required

To temper the chocolate, see page 142.

FROM THE STORES

21 oz (600 g) dark couverture chocolate 55% cocoa, or milk chocolate 35% to 40% cocoa

KITCHEN UTENSILS

Chocolate chicken molds (or rabbits, eggs, etc.)
Cotton balls
Electronic thermometer
Ladle
Flat brush
Clips
Finely meshed rack

DIRECTIONS

For the mold

◉ The first step is to carefully clean the insides of the molds with cotton balls: this removes any dust or impurities, as well as traces of fat left by the cocoa butter from previous use.

◉ After tempering your chocolate, use a brush dipped in the tempered, liquid chocolate (88°F or 31°C for dark, 86°F or 30°C for milk) to line the inside of each mold with a thin, even coat of chocolate. Scrape any excess from the edges. Leave to crystallize (harden) for several minutes at room temperature (68°F/20°C). Repeat this process twice (or three times if the molds are large). After the final layer, scrape the edges, put the two parts together and hold in place with the clips. Leave to solidify.

◉ Turn the mold over and, using a ladle, fill it half full with chocolate through the hole in the bottom. Turn it upside down over the container so that as much as possible runs out. Place the mold on the rack and leave for about 10 minutes. Scrape the edges around the hole and refrigerate the mold for around 45 minutes.

◉ Remove the clips, then use the tip of a sharp knife to carefully separate the two halves of the mold. Keep the chocolate shapes in a dry place at a temperature of about 61°F (16°C).

A **word** from **Gilles** Marchal

When making chocolate shapes at home, I recommend that you take your time and scrupulously apply one of the methods described on page 142. These are the same techniques that chocolate makers follow to the letter: melting the chocolate first and then working with it, being sure to respect the temperature chart. This is called tempering. It's the best way to obtain glossy, pliable shapes and decoration. Molds come in different types of materials: the oldest are made of polished tin, whereas today's models are made either of hard, heat-molded plastic or polycarbonate. Another way to vary the presentation that children will love involves filling the mold with marshmallows, fruit jellies, or nougatine—and then standing it up on a dish. Carefully pour hot milk flavored with vanilla into the dish, and let the chicken melt.

Tempering Chocolate

PRACTICAL SUPPLIES

For tempering, depending on the technique you choose:

Tablage technique:
Bain-marie and mixing bowl
Stainless steel spatula
Rubber spatula
Marble slab (if possible)

Seeding technique:
Bain-marie

Microwave technique:
Microwave-safe plastic container
Microwave

DIRECTIONS

How can I make my chocolate glossy?

Good, high-quality chocolate should be smooth and glossy. When you try to melt chocolate at home to make a topping, a fruit or nut coating, or a mold (Easter eggs for example), the chocolate frequently turns out grainy and dull and takes a long time to harden.

Let me divulge the chocolatier's secret: for chocolate to solidify quickly and turn out smooth and glossy, the cook has to follow a temperature chart to the closest degree—or the chocolate may not turn out at all!

What makes chocolate glossy?

Chocolate is made up partly of cocoa butter, which contains several types of fat molecules. For chocolate to be glossy, all of the molecules in the cocoa butter must go through a very important phase: crystallization. This is what allows the fat content in chocolate to harden into a stable form. However, different types of molecules in the cocoa butter crystallize at different temperatures. That's why chocolate needs to be made following a specific temperature chart, so that each of the molecules can go through crystallization in turn. The process is called tempering.

Tablage technique

1. In a bain-marie, melt all of the chocolate to the melting temperature (temperature no. 1).
2. Pour three-quarters of the chocolate onto a marble slab (marble does not absorb heat so it will help to lower the temperature of your chocolate).

3. Knead the chocolate over the marble using a long spatula (like the type used for crepes) until it reaches the crystallization temperature (temperature no. 2). This completes the tablage phase.
4. Add this chocolate back into the remaining quarter-portion in the bowl and mix to obtain a uniform temperature.

Warm in the mixing bowl for another 2 or 3 seconds to bring the chocolate to the tempering temperature (temperature no. 3). If the temperature is not reached, repeat the process as necessary.

Important! The temperature of the chocolate rises very quickly at this stage; always keep a close eye on your chocolate!

The chocolate is now ready to use for coating chocolate treats (pralines or ganaches), making molds (Easter eggs, rabbits, chickens, Santa Clauses, etc.) and chocolate bars, or dipping various fruits and nuts.

Tip: If you don't have a marble slab to cool your chocolate to temperature no. 2, you can still use this technique; you just have to be patient and wait until the chocolate's temperature drops, kneading it regularly.

Seeding technique

1. In a bain-marie, melt two-thirds of the chocolate, broken into pieces, to the melting temperature (temperature no. 1).
2. Once it reaches temperature no. 1, pour the remaining third of the chocolate pieces into the melted chocolate and stir to obtain an even consistency.

3. Check the temperature: if it is below temperature no. 3, reheat the chocolate slightly in the bain-marie to reach the correct temperature; if it is above temperature no. 3, add more pieces of couverture chocolate until it reaches temperature no. 3 (do not add any water to the chocolate).

Microwave technique
This is the simplest and least traditional technique, but also the one that requires the most attention to changing temperatures. It's the easiest to do at home.
1. Break up the chocolate and place it in a microwave-safe, plastic container.
2. Heat the chocolate in the microwave on the lowest setting (300 watts), stirring regularly until it reaches temperature no. 3. If you have an electronic thermometer, check the temperature; it is important not to exceed 89°F (31 to 32°C).

THE TEMPERATURE CHART

The temperature chart varies depending on the type of couverture chocolate you use: dark, milk, or "white." **Important!** Your chocolate must never exceed temperature no. 3 after going through the preceding stages.

	TEMPERATURE NO. 1 Melting	TEMPERATURE NO. 2 Crystallization	TEMPERATURE NO. 3 Tempering
DARK CHOCOLATE 55% cocoa	122°F/50°C	84°F/28–29°C	89°F/31–32°C
MILK CHOCOLATE 35% cocoa	113°F/45°C	82°F/27–28°C	86°F/30°C
WHITE "CHOCOLATE"	104°F/40°C	80°F/26–27°C	84°F/29°C

Glossary

The greatest satisfaction in making a recipe comes when the result is both delicious and visually appetizing. Success starts with the attention and time that you spend choosing the best ingredients: their freshness, their quality, and their flavor.

Before you start baking a cake, making chocolates, or preparing a dish, it is essential that you read the entire recipe to ensure that you understand it clearly and that you are not missing any of the required ingredients or equipment. That way, you have the best possible chance of producing a result you can be proud of. Some recipes require a little more attention or special equipment, such as an electronic thermometer, sheets of acetate, a piping bag, or a few molds… but just as in art, the more colors you use, the livelier the painting. The faster, simpler recipes must be followed with the same care and attention to the directions, but they demand just an ounce of common sense and very little equipment. It's up to you to decide which recipes will suit you best and fit in with your guests' particular tastes and preferences.

For more than thirty years, we at La Maison du Chocolat have represented the standard in the art of subtly combining this brown gold with fresh cream and flavors from all four corners of the globe. Our cocoa comes from the best plantations and is transformed, just like a bunch of grapes is turned into an exceptional wine, by a specialist in the industry: the *couverturier*. I compare these experts to winemakers, stockbreeders, or tree growers. As for chocolatiers, we are like trained sommeliers or chefs, constantly seeking flavor, creativity, and subtlety in our choice of cocoas, which we use to create our own recipes and develop the tastes so central to our work at La Maison du Chocolat.

Indeed, the origin of the cocoa beans is the main factor in giving a chocolate its rich aroma. Of course, it must be combined with a process that respects the ingredient. From harvesting and processing the cocoa beans to selecting the best ones according to the flavors we are looking for, our couverturier, Valrhona, undertakes the quest for quality on our behalf.

Biscuit: the French name for a sponge cake, in which the eggs are separated, the yolks and whites beaten separately and then folded together with a little flour.

Chocolatier: a professional craftsman who creates chocolate confectionery, sweets, and other treats using couverture chocolate with pure cocoa butter. At La Maison du Chocolat, all of our chocolatiers, or chocolate makers, are professionally trained in producing chocolate.

Coating: each chocolate is coated with a thin layer of milk or dark chocolate to add crunch and protect the quality of the chocolate filling. At La Maison du Chocolat, all of our chocolates are covered in a very fine coating before our chocolate makers decorate each one by hand. The specific decoration for each chocolate is its signature and makes it possible to identify the flavor.

Cocoa beans: each fresh pod contains about fifty beans. After they are fermented, dried, and roasted, they are crushed to produce nibs. At this stage, you can use them in your sauces or to add crunch to your recipes.

Nibs ground to a powder and partially defatted become cocoa powder. When pressed, cocoa beans produce both cocoa butter and cocoa paste.

Cocoa pod: the fruit of the cocoa tree. There are three varieties in the world: Forastero, Trinitario, and Criollo, the rarest variety.

Couverture chocolate: the best kind of chocolate, the raw material used by professionals. The name comes from the fact that it is used to cover (and fill) all types of "chocolate."

Couverturier: an expert in producing couverture chocolate. From choosing and buying beans at the plantation to transforming them into bars of chocolate, couverturiers take the time to scrupulously follow the steps needed to produce exceptional chocolate.

Dark chocolate: a mixture of cocoa paste, cocoa butter, and sugar. It varies between 55% and 99%. 100% refers to "pure cocoa paste" that contains neither sugar nor cocoa butter.

Flan powder/pastry cream powder: a natural starch used to thicken flans and pastry creams.

Fruit nectar: whole, blended fruit. Coulis: whole, blended fruit, sometimes strained, and slightly sweetened. Juice: liquid produced by extracting and then straining the flavored water from fruit.

Fruit pectin: a gelling agent for jams and jellies.

Ganache: a specialty of La Maison du Chocolat; refers to one type of chocolate filling. It is extremely simple to produce, but only a true master can combine deft skill and the complex choice of ingredients to achieve the perfect balance.

Ganache cream: a softer ganache than the variety used in chocolates, it contains more cream and can be spread over bread, toasted brioche, cakes, cookies, and the like.

Glucose: used in confectionery and chocolate making to prevent sugar from crystallizing when cooking sugar syrups (fruit jellies, caramels, etc.). It can be found in specialty cake-making stores.

Gold leaf: made of precious metal that is edible in small quantities, these leaves are so thin that they can be crushed to dust then disappear in the palm of your hand. They are used frequently at La Maison du Chocolat to add a touch of luxury to certain pastries and haute couture pieces.

Infusion: soaking a spice, herb, vanilla bean, or tea in a hot liquid, such as cream, milk, or water. Steeping times vary depending on the intended flavor.

Meringue: there are three types of meringue: Swiss, Italian, and French.

  Swiss: egg whites and sugar heated and whisked together at 120°F (50°C), generally used to cover lemon tarts.

  Italian: sugar is cooked to a syrup at 260°F (125°C) and poured over stiff egg whites; this meringue is generally used to lighten fruit mousses and creams.

  French: superfine granulated sugar is gradually poured over stiff egg whites, and then confectioners' sugar is added; generally used for baked meringues (*vacherin*, for example).

Milk chocolate: a mixture of cocoa paste, cocoa butter, sugar, milk, and sometimes vanilla. It contains between 33% and 45% cocoa.

Praline: a mixture of roasted nuts (almonds and hazelnuts) and cooked, caramelized sugar, crushed to varying degrees of fineness to obtain a grainy praline (traditional praline) or a smooth paste (fine praline). It is one type of chocolate filling. It can also be made using pecans, peanuts, coconut, etc.

Pure cocoa butter: this appellation is an indication of quality. Our love and respect for the ingredient means that we naturally respect the appellation.

Tempering: a process of heating and cooking chocolate to create a smooth texture, glossy shine, and crisp bite. See page 142 for tempering instructions.

Truffle paste: a frothy ganache frequently used to produce lighter truffles.

Valrhona: a supplier of the best cocoas, which are used to produce exceptional, single-origin chocolates (from Venezuela, Mexico, Ecuador, Trinidad, Ghana, Madagascar, and Java, to name a few locations).

  A Valrhona sourcer travels around the world with the sole objective of uncovering the best cocoa plantations along the equator, between the Tropic of Cancer and the Tropic of Capricorn.

White "chocolate": the name is somewhat misleading, because white chocolate does not contain any cocoa paste, only cocoa butter, sugar, milk, and vanilla. At La Maison du Chocolat, we use it only for decoration.

Glossary

Acetate sheets: usually used to create the most delicate types of decoration (see photo of the chocolatier's hand-bag, page 118). You can find sheets of the material in art supply stores. A new, perfectly smooth transparency for an overhead projector will work as well.

Dry ice: water transformed from a liquid state to a solid state through contact with nitrogen. With a very low temperature of -290°F (-180°C), dry ice is used for a spectacular effect and the presentation of certain desserts (see photo page 136). Dry ice should be handled with great care because it is so cold.

Electric mixer: used to mix larger quantities of ingredients than a whisk, the electric mixer is available as a hand or stand mixer, depending on the power you require.

Electronic scales: just as impor-tant as the recipe. In pastry making, everything is weighed, often down to the gram. That's why we call the area where our pastry chefs bake their cakes and other specialties the laboratory.

Electronic thermometer: this has become a necessary piece of equip-ment for some recipes, especially for perfecting (or tempering) chocolate to be used in molds. It is also useful for making custards, caramels, fruit jel-lies, icing, and any other recipe that demands precise temperatures.

Food processor: an electric kitchen appliance with interchangeable blades and different speed options for processing.

Immersion blender: generally used to blend soups, this hand-held blender is also useful for mashing fresh fruit to produce a pulp or coulis and for gently mixing warm ganache to make it com-pletely smooth by creating a perfect emulsion.

Microplane grater: not to be con-fused with a zester or a paring knife. American Microplane graters can be used to produce very fine zests from citrus fruits; zesters generally produce threads, and paring knives strips.

Piping bag: these are commonly found in kitchens, but you can also use a plastic freezer bag. Just use scissors to cut one of the corners of the bag to the size indicated by the tip number (for example, a ⁵⁄₁₆-in (8-mm) opening for a No. 8 tip). If you have tips, you can also place them in your freezer bag.

Template or stencil: used as a guide to give a precise shape to melted choco-late, *biscuit* or other dough, or any product you need to spread out. You can create your own stencils by cutting them out from a plastic lid, sheet of acetate, or cardboard for food use.

Whisk: a wire whip used to whip or blend small quantities of ingredients such as eggs or cream.

My Favorite Foodie Discoveries

These are a few of my favorite places, not only because of their delicious sweet and savory dishes, but also because of the people who prepare them. When I like a dish, I can't help but love its creator.

NEW YORK

▣ L'Atelier Joël Robuchon
Four Seasons Hotel, 57 East 57th Street,
New York, NY 10022
Phone: 212-350-6658
Scallops in their shell with seaweed butter
Golden sugar sphere, vanilla ice cream,
saffron mousse

▣ Café Boulud
20 East 76th Street, New York, NY 10021
Phone: 212-772-2600
Biscuit and gravy pork, foie gras, black truffle,
creamed spinach, sauce Périgourdine
Roasted rib eye, pommes Pont Neuf, bacon-
wrapped haricots verts, bordelaise sauce

▣ La Grenouille
3 East 52nd Street, New York, NY 10022
Phone: 212-752-1495
Steamed cod with anchovies, capers, shallot crust,
and lemon zest
Warm bitter chocolate torte

▣ The Modern
The Museum of Modern Art, 9 West 53rd Street,
New York, NY 10019
Phone: 212-333-1220
Squab and foie gras croustillant with caramelized
sugar jus and farm vegetables
Baba Grand Marnier, roasted mango, vanilla ice
cream, lime sabayon

▣ Spice Market
403 West 13th Street, New York, NY 10014
Phone: 212-675-2322
Steamed red snapper with mushrooms, ginger,
scallions, and tarragon
Valrhona chocolate and pecan tart, spiced pear
sorbet

▣ Via Quadronno
25 East 73rd Street, New York, NY 10075
Phone: 212-650-2880
Milanese-style veal, with tuna caper sauce
Mini panettone

MONTREAL

◉ Queue de Cheval
1221 René Levesque Ouest, Montreal PQ H3G 171
Phone: 514-390-0090
Drunken beef with cream of spinach brulée
Fresh berry shortcake

LONDON

◉ L'Atelier Joël Robuchon
12–15 West Street, Soho, London WC2H 9NE
Phone: +44 207 010 8600
Scallops with black truffle and fondant leeks
Warm passion fruit soufflé

◉ L'Oranger
5 St James Street, London SW1A 1EF
Phone: +44 207 839 3774
Seared salmon with gingerbread
Single cream quenelle
Menton lemon macaron

PARIS

◉ Bath's
25, rue Bayen, 75017 Paris
Phone: +33 1 45 74 74 74
Roasted wild duck, puréed peas, savory
vinaigrette
Caramel millefeuille, vanilla cream, wild
strawberries

◉ Le Bristol
112, rue du Faubourg-Saint-Honoré, 75008 Paris
Phone: +33 1 53 43 43 00
Macaroni stuffed with black truffle, artichoke,
and foie gras
Rare "Nyangbo" chocolate with a sweet wafer

◉ La Crèmerie
9, rue des Quatre-Vents, 75006 Paris
Phone: +33 1 43 54 99 30
Burrata, olive oil, fresh basil
Molten chocolate cake

◉ Le Gaigne
12, rue Pecquay, 75004 Paris
Phone: +33 1 44 59 86 72
Hake, julienned snap peas, diced cuttlefish,
piquillos
Tropical fruit, frozen passion fruit parfait,
coconut velouté

La **Maison** du **Chocolat Store** Locations

PARIS

◉ 225, rue du Faubourg-Saint-Honoré, 75008 Paris
Phone: +33 1 42 27 39 44
◉ 52, rue François-Ier, 75008 Paris
Phone: +33 1 47 23 38 25
◉ 8, boulevard de la Madeleine, 75009 Paris
Phone: +33 1 47 42 86 52
◉ 19, rue de Sèvres, 75006 Paris
Phone: +33 1 45 44 20 40
◉ 120, avenue Victor-Hugo, 75116 Paris
Phone: +33 1 40 67 77 83
◉ Printemps de la Maison, 2nd floor,
64, boulevard Haussmann, 75009 Paris
Phone: +33 1 42 82 50 00
◉ Carrousel du Louvre, 99, rue de Rivoli, 75001 Paris
Phone: +33 1 42 97 13 50

CANNES

◉ 87–89, rue d'Antibes (rue des Gabres), 06400 Cannes
Phone: +33 4 93 94 44 70

LONDON

◉ 45–46 Piccadilly, London W1J 0DS
Phone: +44 207 287 8500
◉ Harrods, Knightsbridge, London SW1 XXL
Phone: +44 207 730 1234

NEW YORK

◉ 1018 Madison Avenue, New York, NY 10075
Phone: 212-744-7117
◉ 30 Rockefeller Center, New York, NY 10020
Phone: 212-265-9404
◉ 63 Wall Street, New York, NY 10005
Phone: 212-952-1123

TOKYO

◉ Hanae Mori Building, 1F, 3-6-1, Kita-Aoyama, Minato-ku, Tokyo 107-0061
Phone: +81 3 3499 2168
◉ New Kokusai Building, 1F, 3-4-1, Marunouchi, Chiyoda-ku, Tokyo 100-0005
Phone: +81 3 3201 6006

HONG KONG

◉ Shop 246, Level 2 The Mall, Pacific Place, s88 Queensway, Admiralty, Hong Kong
Phone: +852 2522 2010
◉ Shop 2040A, Elements, 1 Austin West Road, Tsim Sha Tsui, Kowloon, Hong Kong
Phone: +852 2196 8333

www.lamaisonduchocolat.com

Sources

Artgato
Small chocolate molds.
1, avenue du Docteur-Netter,
75012 Paris
Phone: +33 1 44 73 93 13

Café Verlet
Aromatic coffees.
250, rue Saint-Honoré, 75001 Paris
Phone: +33 1 42 60 91 29

Comptoir de la Gastronomie
Foie gras.
34, rue Montmartre, 75001 Paris
Phone: +33 1 42 33 31 32

Eli's Manhattan
Spices, flour, baking ingredients.
1411 Third Avenue, New York, NY 10028
Phone: 212-717-8100

G Detou
Bourbon vanilla and gold leaf.
58, rue Tiquetonne, 75002 Paris
Phone: +33 1 42 36 54 67

La Grande Épicerie de Paris
Wine paired with Chistera ganache.
38, rue de Sèvres, 75007 Paris
Phone: +33 1 44 39 80 00

Kalustyan's
Spices.
123 Lexington Avenue,
New York, NY 10016
Phone: 212-685-3451

Maison Colom
Berries.
150, avenue Victor-Hugo, 75016 Paris
Phone: +33 1 47 27 90 30

Le Monde de la Truffe
Perigord black truffles.
4, rue Molière, 91380 Chilly-Mazarin
Phone: +33 1 64 48 20 47

Le Monde des Épices
Spices.
30, rue François-Miron, 75004 Paris
Phone: +33 1 42 72 66 23

Mora
Baking and kitchen utensils.
13, rue Montmartre, 75001 Paris
Phone: +33 1 45 08 19 24

New York Cake and Baking Supply
Small chocolate molds, baking supplies.
56 West 22nd Street,
New York, NY 10010
212-675-253
www.nycake.com

La Nivernaise
Veal sweetbreads.
99, rue du Faubourg-Saint-Honoré,
75008 Paris
Phone: +33 1 43 59 11 02

Oliviers & Co.
Corsican olive oil from the Domaine de
Marquiliani.
90, rue de Montorgueil, 75002 Paris
Phone: +33 1 44 82 62 28
info@oliviers-co.com

Tamayura
Japanese Matcha green tea.
www.tamayura.fr

Valrhona
Chocolate.
14, avenue du Président-Roosevelt,
26600 Tain-l'Hermitage
Phone: +33 1 75 07 90 62
www.valrhona.com

Les Vergers Saint-Eustache
Exotic fruit.
1, rue de Provence, 94150 Rungis
Phone: +33 1 41 73 74 75

Williams-Sonoma
Baking and kitchen utensils.
www.williams-sonoma.com

Zabar's
Spices, flour, baking ingredients.
2245 Broadway, New York NY 10024
Phone: 212-787-2000

Acknowledgments

▣ Véronique Durruty, not only for her enthusiasm, joie de vivre, and passion for chocolate, but above all for the sweet and savory works of art featured in this book. Her daughter Nikita and her friend Augusta, for their help and testing during our photo shoots.

▣ The entire team of pastry chefs and chocolatiers at La Maison du Chocolat, especially Alex Bodereau, Ronan Garcia, and Nicolas Cloiseau.

▣ David Casiez, without whom I would never have been able to take the time off to create this book and who prepared all the ingredients used in these recipes.

▣ The entire team led by Marie Stoclet-Bardon, particularly Aurélie Rousseaux-Gubri. Without their enormous contributions, this book would not be what it is today.

▣ Geoffroy d'Anglejan, Managing Director, and the entire management committee at La Maison du Chocolat, for their support and encouragement throughout the process of making these recipes.

▣ All of the employees in Tokyo, New York, Hong Kong, London, Cannes, and Paris who make up the extended international family of La Maison du Chocolat.

▣ Robert Linxe, founder of La Maison du Chocolat, and his wife Gisèle, who we are honored to follow down the chocolatey trail they first blazed thirty years ago.

▣ Camille Lescure, Mona Oren, Élodie Rousselot, Claire Colin, Camille Hammerer, and Vanessa Batut, for their inspiring work and the discussions we shared.

▣ Michèle Carles, one of the top food journalists, who has supported La Maison du Chocolat since very early on, for her incredibly touching foreword.

▣ Lucile Jouret for her pertinent comments, Armelle Heron for her keen eye, Laure Lamendin for her patience, and Éditions Aubanel for their confidence.

▣ Pierre Costet, a sourcer of high quality cocoa at Valrhona, who introduces me to the best plantations and shares his rich chocolate culture.

▣ My chef friends Éric Fréchon and Christophe Bacquié for their unusual suggestions.

▣ My pastry-making comrades Laurent Jeannin, Christophe Felder, and Frédéric Bau.

▣ Le Bristol hotel, a true friend.

▣ My best and most loyal former colleagues: Wesley Tulwa, Frédéric Després, Vincent Doidy, and Fabrice Lebourdat.

▣ The Club des Sucrés for the stunning, ephemeral creations and friendship that bind us together.

▣ My parents, Pierre and Odette, for sharing their recipes and supporting me right from the start.

▣ My brother, sister, and brother-in-law for their love of pâtisserie; Jean and Marie for their new recipes.

▣ And, of course, I could never forget my own family: Gina, my wife, and my children Théo, Matthieu, and Lisa, who accept the long absences I take to follow my passion and always welcome me home with their biggest smiles.

VÉRONIQUE DURRUTY WOULD LIKE TO THANK:

▣ Gilles Marchal, for allowing me to work so happily in his epicurean world and for introducing me to so many flavors.

▣ Cyril, David, Greg, and the entire team of pastry chefs and chocolate makers who worked behind the scenes to prepare these recipes.

▣ Mona Oren, Camille Lescure, Vanessa Batut, Claire Colin, Élodie Rousselot, and Camille Hammerer for their camera-friendly creations.

▣ Emmanuelle Vainqueur, who lent her grace, kindness, and physique of a Nubian princess to Élodie's breastplate; Isabelle Théviot, who delicately adorned it with gold; and Zoé Pignollet and Marie-Liesse of La Bouillerie, for their help with the shoot.

▣ As'Art for lending us their rare and beautiful objects (such as the incense holder used for the truffles, see page 16). Founded in 1991 for an initial long-term development project in Kenya, As'Art later joined forces with other humanitarian projects and causes in Mozambique, Ethiopia, and later South Africa. (asart@wanadoo.fr)

▣ Anne Serroy, Isabelle Raynaud, and Laure Lamendin, who entrusted this project to me; Lucile Jouret; Sophie Gallet for her efficiency and her warm smile; and, of course, Marie-Hélène Lafin and Isabelle Hortal, whose meticulous work on project after project is what brings out the magic in my images.

▣ The employees at La Maison du Chocolat's workshops and boutiques for their friendly welcome, with particular thanks to Marie Stocklet-Bardon and Aurélie Rousseaux-Gubri.

▣ Nikita and Augusta, for their work both as assistants and as highly motivated and effective tasters.

▣ And Krishna, the god who doesn't believe that gluttony is a mortal sin!

To learn more about Véronique Durruty's work, visit http://durrutyguedjphoto.free.fr

Published in 2009 by Stewart, Tabori & Chang
An imprint of ABRAMS

Cataloging-in-Publication Data has been applied for
and may be obtained from the Library of Congress.

ISBN 978-1-58479-800-2

Aubanel Edition
Coordinating editor: Laure Lamendin
Artist recruitment and coordination: Vanessa Batut
and Camille Hammerer
Editor and proofreader: Armelle Heron
Graphic design and production: Lucile Jouret
Translation, English-language edition: I.D.O. Paris21

STC Edition
Project manager: Magali Veillon
Recipe editor: Leah Stewart
Designer: Shawn Dahl
Production manager: Jules Thomson

The text of this book was composed in Proxima Nova.

Printed and bound in Singapore
10 9 8 7 6 5 4 3 2 1

For more information about the work of the
artists presented in this book:

Vanessa Batut
vanessabatut@yahoo.fr

Claire Colin
www.myspace.com/dentellegourmande
cclairecoco@voila.fr

Camille Hammerer
camille.hammerer@free.fr

Camille Lescure
www.camillelescure.com
camille.lescure@gmail.com

Mona Oren
www.monaoren.com
monaoren@gmail.com

Élodie Rousselot
www.elodierousselot.com
rousselotelod@hotmail.com

ABRAMS
THE **ART OF BOOKS** SINCE 1949

115 West 18th Street
New York, NY 10011
www.abramsbooks.com